What Learning Looks Like... Pre-school

# Creative Development

Hilary White

## Contents

# About this book

This book takes a close look at one of the six areas of learning in the curriculum guidelines across the United Kingdom - Creative Development in England and Wales, Expressive and Aesthetic Development in Scotland and Creative/Aesthetic Development in Northern Ireland.

## Guidance and good practice

The author explains what the area of learning consists of, what the jargon means and how it applies to the various settings in the Foundation Stage of education - children aged between three and five.

There are four different curriculum bodies across the United Kingdom - the Qualifications and Curriculum Authority (QCA) in England; the Curriculum and Assessment Authority for Wales (Awdurdod Cwricwlwm Ac Asesu Cymru); the Scottish Consultative Council on the Curriculum; and the Northern Ireland Council for the Curriculum Examinations and Assessment. Each has a different statement relating to the desired curriculum for young children. However, although there are some differences in terminology and some slight variations in emphasis, good practice in one country is still considered good practice in another.

As well as giving theoretical guidance - albeit in practical terms - the book also offers suggestions for activities which can be used to deliver the curriculum requirements.

## Practical activities

All these activities should be considered as merging into the normal life of the early years setting. The book stresses the importance of play and looks at how the different areas of learning are linked. The activities are not prescriptive and should not be seen as tasks to complete. They are designed to be manageable and fun.

There are suggestions for 15 activities. Some are simple and basic activities which need few resources. Others are deliberately more challenging. Each can be used in some form with children at different stages of development.

The activities are planned to cover all the Creative Development Early Learning Goals (ELGs). Many of the ELGs overlap and interrelate with one another. The activities therefore often fulfil more than one goal.

All the activities follow the same format:

- ❑ The activity is introduced.
- ❑ Links are given with the Stepping Stones (from the *Curriculum Guidance for the Foundation Stage*). Related Early Learning Goals are in a box.
- ❑ Resources are listed under 'What you will need'.
- ❑ Suggestions are made for any preparations required before you start ('Getting ready').
- ❑ The activities are explained ('What to do') and, where possible, suggestions are given to suit different ages or developmental levels. These are kept very broad, with references only to 'older children' and 'younger children'.
- ❑ Ideas for assessment are also given in a box.
- ❑ Where relevant, suggestions are made for further activities (under 'Other activities'). These are linked to the theme and can be implemented alongside the main activity.

## Ages and stages

All children develop at different rates. Children within the Foundation Stage, move along a continuum and their progress will not necessarily be steady or uniform. We must not focus on age appropriate activities but developmentally appropriate activities. Within your group you will probably have children working at various levels.

The activities in this book are only ideas and should not be seen as prescriptive models! You may want to adapt and change them to make them more appropriate for the group of children you are teaching.

Any suggestions as to what a child should be able to do must be regarded as flexible. While it is useful to have guidelines to help you plan appropriate activities for your group, it is important to remember that children vary in the pace at which they develop. The main aim of the early years worker should always be to observe, assess, value and cater for each child as an individual.

## Planning

A planning chart has been included for support and guidance but we would encourage you to adapt this readily to meet your own needs and circumstances.

There are seven books in this series, and although each book can be used by itself, they are designed to fit together so that the whole learning framework is covered.

The seven titles are:

- ❑ Personal, Social and Emotional Development
- ❑ Language and Literacy
- ❑ Mathematical Development
- ❑ Knowledge and Understanding of the World: Geography and History
- ❑ Knowledge and Understanding of the World: Science and Technology.
- ❑ Physical Development
- ❑ Creative Development

All of these books carry some activities based on common themes which, when used together, will give enough ideas for a cross-curricular topic over a half or even a full term.

The common themes are:

- ❑ Seasons
- ❑ Water
- ❑ Colour
- ❑ All about me
- ❑ People who help us

All the books together provide an outline of the learning which should be taking place in the Foundation Stage.

## Assessment

Each activity includes an assessment box. Assessment involves two distinct activities:

- ❑ The gathering of information about the child's capabilities.
- ❑ Making a judgement based on this information.

Assessment should not take place in isolation. We assess to meet individual needs and ensure progress. The following tips may help your assessment to be more effective.

- ❑ Assessment is a continuous process. It should be systematic to ensure all children are observed on a regular basis.
- ❑ Assessment should always start with the child. The first steps in providing appropriate provision is by sensitively observing children to identify their learning needs.
- ❑ Assessment should not take place to see how much the child has learned but to plan appropriately for future activities.
- ❑ You should be a participant in the assessment process, interacting and communicating with the child.

The main way of assessing the young child is through careful observation.

Observations should:

- ❑ Record both the positive and negative behaviour shown.
- ❑ Be long enough to make the child's behaviour meaningful.
- ❑ Record only what you see and not what you think you have seen or heard.
- ❑ Be clear - before you begin be sure you know what you want to observe.
- ❑ Be organised - plan ahead, otherwise it will not happen.

What Learning Looks Like...

Creative Development

# National guidelines

England, Scotland, Wales and Northern Ireland each have their own set of guidelines for pre-school settings. Although the expectations are broadly similar in all four documents, there are differences in detail and format. The Scottish Curriculum Framework is more comprehensive than the Welsh guidelines, whereas the Northern Ireland document includes a useful general description of how learning can be expected to progress for each curriculum area.

## The English Early Learning Goals

The most recently published English document is called *Curriculum Guidance for the Foundation Stage.* The document includes the Early Learning Goals, which set out what most children should have achieved by the end of the Foundation Stage. The Foundation Stage runs from the age of three to the end of the child's first year of compulsory schooling (the reception class). The child's age at the end of reception can vary considerably, from 5.0 in the case of an August birthday to 5.11 if the child was born in September. This should always be taken into account when assessing the child's progress and development throughout the Foundation Stage.

Although the goals are not a curriculum in themselves, they cover the six curriculum areas of Personal, Social and Emotional Development; Communication, Language and Literacy; Mathematical Development; Knowledge and Understanding of the World; Creative Development and Physical Development.

Each goal also has a number of Stepping Stones. These identify the knowledge, skills, understanding and attitudes that lead towards the goals. The Stepping Stones are not age related, although it is broadly assumed that the earlier ones will apply to the child at three while the final stepping stone (the Early Learning Goal itself) describes the child's achievement at rising six. The Stepping Stones include some useful illustrative examples of what children might do and how the early years worker can support and consolidate learning.

The Early Learning Goals for Creative Development cover music and singing, dance, art, craft and modelling, story telling and imaginative and role play. There is also an emphasis on the creative importance of the senses, with the goal requiring children to respond in a variety of ways to what they see, hear, smell, touch and feel.

Some of the goals have a clear link with a particular creative activity, such as the music related 'recognise and explore how sounds can be changed, sing simple songs from memory, recognise repeated sounds and sound patterns and match movements to music'. Others have a broader application, such as the use of imagination in various creative activities, or the ability to choose suitable tools to 'express and communicate their ideas, thoughts and feelings'.

For a more detailed look at the English Creative Development goals, turn to pages 7-13, 'The area of learning explained'.

## The Scottish Curriculum Framework

The Scottish Curriculum Framework uses the title Expressive and Aesthetic Development for its creative area of learning. Like the English Early Learning Goals, it covers music and singing, art, craft and modelling, dance and role play.

The major difference between the

Scottish and English guidelines lies in the age specifications, with the Scottish Framework aimed at children from three to five rather than rising six.

Another difference is the way in which the guidelines correspond with the separate areas of music, art, craft, dance and role play. Whereas some English goals encompass a number of different activities or apply across the board (such as 'respond in a variety of ways to what they see, hear, smell, touch and feel'), the Scottish guidelines each link with a specific creative activity. The connection with art, craft and modelling is obvious in 'investigate and use a variety of media and techniques such as painting, drawing, printing and modelling with fabrics, clay and other materials'. The connection with music is clearly stated in 'make music by singing, clapping and playing percussion instruments'.

This format makes the Scottish framework easy to use as a basis for planning across the curriculum. It does not, however, place much emphasis on the interrelated nature of different creative activities.

Unlike the English goals, none of the Scottish guidelines focus on the imagination, although this aspect of creativity is mentioned in the general introduction. However, the communicative and emotional aspects of creative activity are well catered for with guidelines such as:

❑ express thoughts and feelings in pictures, paintings and models;

❑ use verbal and non-verbal language in role play;

❑ use instruments by themselves and in groups to invent music which expresses their thoughts and feelings.

Many of the statements are quite broad and refer to the children simply experiencing the activities and using different elements, tools and instruments. For example:

❑ investigate and use a variety of media and techniques such as painting, drawing, printing and modelling with fabrics, clay and other materials;

❑ make music by singing, clapping and playing percussion instruments;

❑ participate in simple dances and singing games.

The Scottish framework as a whole comes across as less prescriptive and goal orientated than the English curriculum guidance. These differences are not quite so marked in Creative Development as in some other areas of learning - in keeping with the open-ended nature of most creative activities.

## The Northern Ireland Curricular Guidance for Pre-School Education

The *Northern Ireland Curricular Guidance for Pre-school Education* uses the title Creative/Aesthetic Development to describe this area of learning.

The format of the guidance is different to the English, Scottish and Welsh. It reads as a description of why and how a child should develop creatively rather than presenting a list of separate statements, goals or guidelines.

The section on Creative/Aesthetic Development opens with a thoughtful overview of the learning area, focussing on the role of creative play to 'assist emotional development, promote aesthetic awareness', provide an 'avenue for self-expression' and, most important of all, 'experience the joy of achievement'.

The next part divides creative play activity under the headings 'Painting and drawing'; 'Paper, card, wood, fabrics and scrap materials'; 'Malleable materials' and 'Music'. Each heading is followed by a number of activities, skills and concepts. For example:

❑ working with paper of different colours, shapes, textures and sizes ('Painting and drawing');

❑ work(ing) with materials of different textures which will offer them sensory experiences ('Paper, card, wood, fabrics and scrap materials');

❑ opportunities to work with large amounts of clay and dough ('Malleable materials');

❑ participate in simple music activities such as singing and listening to music ('Music').

The third section describes the characteristics and skills that most children who have received appropriate pre-school education should display. These include:

❑ the ability to explore a range of materials and appreciate colour, texture, shape and sound;

❑ the ability to express and communicate ideas, feelings and imagination;

❑ the ability to make simple representations using a range of materials;

❑ the ability to talk about and value their work and that of other children.

Apart from one or two thin areas (dance, the creative use of language in storytelling, role play) the Northern Ireland guidance covers much the same range and detail as England and Scotland. The emphasis on description rather than listed points may make it a little less easy to use as the basis for planning activities across the creative area of learning. There is no doubt, however, that it captures the spirit and purpose of creative activity for the young child.

## The Welsh Desirable Outcomes for Children's Learning before Compulsory School Age

The introduction to the Welsh Desirable Outcomes emphasises that they are not to be regarded as a self contained check-list. The strength of the document lies in its nature as a clear, simple and comprehensive framework.

The Creative Development section covers:

❑ response to rhythm in music, including the use of instruments and voices;

❑ creating representational images with a range of materials;

❑ making 'choices about colour and medium';

❑ dancing and making 'imitative movements' in response to suggestions;

❑ discussing work, both during and after completion;

❑ starting to enjoy imaginative and role play and drama;

❑ starting to 'observe and appreciate the work of others'.

Two important aspects of Creative Development are only to be found in the Welsh outcomes:

❑ discuss work in progress and completed;

❑ begin to observe and appreciate the work of others.

Although England, Scotland and Northern Ireland touch on these elements, it is only in the Welsh guidance that they are highlighted as distinct goals to work towards.

In comparison with the English, Scottish or Northern Ireland guidance, many of the Welsh outcomes are brief. For example, whereas the English goals identify the visual elements of colour, texture, shape, space and form, the comparable Welsh outcome confines itself to 'make choices about colour and medium'. The Northern Ireland guidance lists musical elements such as different sounds, pitch and rhythm while the corresponding Welsh outcome simply says 'respond to and enjoy rhythm in music'. The Desirable Outcomes for Wales do not provide a detailed set of skills, concepts, knowledge areas or creative elements. For these, the early years worker will have to look elsewhere.

What Learning Looks Like...

**Creative Development**

# The area of learning explained

Creativity is one of the most important aspects of a young child's development. From babyhood, a child gathers skills and information that she can use later in life to create ideas, pictures, sculptures, music, dance, stories .... the list is endless.

We tend to think of creativity as applying to the five main areas of the visual arts, literature, music, dance and drama. While these are central to planning creative activities in your setting, it is worth remembering that creativity comes into play in all aspects of life. The executive business person is being creative when he or she thinks up a new system to solve a marketing problem. The parent is being creative when he or she distracts a crying child with a game. A group of scientists are being creative when they come up with a 'What if ...?' question to test out with an experiment.

Creativity means being able to approach any situation and use whatever skills and knowledge you have at your disposal to come up with a response to that situation.

The Early Learning Goals for Creative Development cover art, music, dance, role play and imaginative play. Many of the goals can be applied to more than one of these areas, highlighting the fact that a creative activity will often draw from more than one art form. For example, movement and music; making puppets for acting out a story; using fabric collage to make role-play props; drawing musical instruments to add to a music display. The goals themselves link with the following areas:

## Developing the senses

If the child is to respond creatively to whatever life asks of her, she needs to have a broad set of experiences to draw from. This is something the Early Learning Goals recognise with the requirement that children should be able to 'respond in a variety of ways to what they see, hear, smell, touch and feel'. Developing all the senses - sight, touch, hearing, smell and taste - is important. Encourage your children to use different senses as part of their everyday exploration of their environment and help them to respond to their sensory experiences.

### Looking

Many of your planned activities will help children to develop their visual sense, but you can also seize one-off opportunities as they come along. If a child expresses interest in a particular object, make sure that you draw attention to the visual aspects - colour, shape and detail. Use colour names with the young ones and introduce words to describe colour with older ones - dark, light, pale, bright, glossy, matt. Use similes - 'It looks like ....' or 'It reminds me of ....'

Even a simple object such as a shell on the nature table presents a host of opportunities to observe and talk about visual qualities - its spiral shape, the tiny spots, the spiky edge, the tortoiseshell pattern that reminds you of the school cat.

Magnifying glasses can be a useful resource. Make them constantly available so that children can get into the habit of using them whenever they want to look closely at something. Novelty items can also be introduced to focus the children's attention on the act of looking; sheets of coloured acetate to look through, sunglasses, kaleidoscopes, an 'insect's eye' viewer, sheet magnifiers and mirrors can all be put out in your setting for the children to explore.

### Listening

Music, singing and listening to stories and tapes are all essential activities when it comes to helping the child develop listening skills. As with looking, you can also watch out for one-off occasions to highlight the act of listening and encourage the children to respond to what they can hear. Traffic, children playing, animals and the weather are all good sources of everyday sounds.

Encourage the children to sit still and listen to the different sounds that surround them. Help them to express their experience through language by introducing 'sound' words - pitter patter, crash, boom, rattle, slam, clap (*Roget's Thesaurus* is a good source of words if you want to expand your own 'sounds' vocabulary.)

Focus on an emotional response to sound by asking the children how a sound makes them feel. Be prepared for a variety of replies. Some individuals want to curl up into a ball at the sound of a fire engine siren whereas others find it exhilarating. If you receive contrasting responses, draw attention to these differences - 'Jonathan puts his fingers in his ears when he hears the fire engine'; 'Jessica feels excited when she hears the fire engine ...' This will help the children discover that reaction to sensory experiences is a personal thing.

### Feeling

Feeling or touching objects gives us lots of information about our environment. Whenever you are looking at a new object or introducing a new activity, encourage the children to explore through their sense of touch. Activities such as model making, collage, cooking, playing musical instruments and looking at objects from the natural world provide a rich variety of textures to enjoy. Introduce 'texture' words - sticky, bumpy, crunchy, crumpled and compare different contrasting tactile experiences such as rough/smooth or wet/dry. Talk about the importance of the sense of touch for those with visual or hearing impairment and show older children Braille and the raised symbols on a cassette recorder (see page 51 for games and activities to help the children focus on and develop their sense of touch.)

### Smelling

This sense is perhaps the least obvious in the human being, although research shows that the sense of smell operates from birth. It is not unusual for even a young child to identify the owner of the stray cardigan because she can link washing powder smells with particular people. Many young children cannot tolerate unpleasant or very strong odours so any planned work on smelling has to be thought about carefully (see page 52 for activities.) As with all the other senses, look out for spontaneous moments - a visitor wearing a beautiful perfume, the smell of the garden after the rain, the smell of cooking, the scent of flowers. Smell can evoke powerful emotional responses - it is often the sensory experience that brings back the most vivid of memories. Pre-school children are unlikely to have developed smell memories but you can still ask them whether they like a smell and how it makes them feel. An odour or scent will often elicit a strong facial expression. Encourage the children to use their faces as part of their response to smell.

If the child can use all her senses to the full, she will end up with a more rounded set of experiences to use in her creative activities. For example, the older child who has looked at, listened to and felt the rain on her face will have lots to bring to a rain inspired painting, dance or musical composition. During the Foundation Stage, the main emphasis should be on encouraging an awareness of looking, listening, touching and smelling, and developing the child's ability to use her senses. You can, however, start to encourage the child to use sensory information in her creative work. Try some of the following:

- ❑ older children can look carefully at a plant or object before drawing what they see (see pages 22-23);
- ❑ children can choose percussion instruments or body percussion movements to express the different sounds they hear (see pages 34-37);
- ❑ children can respond to texture through mime - walking barefoot on a pebbly beach or stroking a soft, fluffy kitten (see pages 60-61);
- ❑ the look, smell and texture of something can all be brought into poems and story making (see pages 54-55).

These are just a few of the ways in which sensory experiences can inform the creative activities of art, music, dance and drama. Similarly, these activities can help the child focus on and explore the fascinating - and fundamental - activities of looking, touching, listening and smelling.

## Exploring colour, texture, form and space

Colour, texture, form and space are some of the main elements that the child comes across through exploring her environment with all her senses. The Early Learning Goals recognise their significance with the statement that children should be able to 'explore colour, texture, shape, form and space in two or three dimensions' by the end of the reception year.

This goal has a particular link with art, craft, design and model making.

### Colour

Exploring colour through art begins from the first moment the child picks up a coloured pencil or wax crayon. Give your very youngest children just two or three colours to work with. This helps them to focus on the difference between the colours without overwhelming them. Older children can be introduced to colour mixing and lightening/darkening colours through painting, sponge printing and superimposing one wax layer over another (see page 21). They can also be encouraged to choose the colour of paper they work on and the type of colours for a particular picture - hot colours, cool colours, pastel colours, bright colours. Juxtaposing different coloured papers in a collage is another means of exploring colour through art. How does the red crepe paper look on a green background as opposed to a white background?

### Texture

Texture is explored every time the child uses a range of different materials for cutting and sticking, or clay and playdough for modelling. Choose materials with contrasting textures for collage - cotton wool, sandpaper, velvet, dried flowers, glossy paper.

Model making gives the child constant experiences of texture, whether it is the slippery, gooey surface of wet clay or the hard, ridged texture of corrugated card. The child can manipulate and change the texture of her model by using tools on the surface of clay or sticking a range of collage materials onto her corrugated card.

## Shape

Shape is an essential aspect of both two- and three-dimensional art. Shape means the outline of an object. From the very beginning, the baby's mark making produces the line that will one day be controlled and formed into the drawing of a shape on paper. Shape is all around us, both geometric shapes and shapes in nature. Puzzles, matching and sorting shape activities, play shapes and picture books are all important ways of helping the child to explore and learn to recognise shape.

In art work, you can give children shapes to decorate, draw around and copy. Even very young children can be given ready-cut shapes or pressed leaves and flowers to use in collage. Sponges and potatoes can be cut into shapes for printing (see pages 24- 25). Older children can be encouraged to look carefully at the shape of an object before drawing or painting that shape on the paper.

## Form

Form also means shape, but without the emphasis on outline. We therefore tend to apply it to three- dimensional models - clay, Plasticene, playdough, salt dough, junk modelling. Different types of material offer the child different ways of exploring form. Clay uses a very hands-on approach. The form can be changed over and over again as the clay is squeezed, smoothed and moulded by the hands. Junk modelling is a little different. The form is constructed through adding pieces one by one with the child having to think about balance and support. Give your children a range of different modelling materials, including construction materials such as building blocks and bricks. Leave little ones free to explore and enjoy the materials. Older ones can be shown techniques for creating a range of different forms, such as rolling sausages, snakes and balls, making thumb pots and coil pots, cutting tiles from clay or other modelling materials (see pages 31-32). As well as giving their imaginations free range with junk modelling, older children can also be set challenges such as building the tallest construction they can manage (see page 33).

## Space

Space is as important to a picture as detail. The whole appearance of a picture changes if the space between the tree and the house is small rather than large. Use collage as a means of encouraging children to explore space in their work. Introduce the idea of laying out the pieces on the background paper and experimenting with the composition before the final sticking. If your children cope well with this activity, you can gradually introduce the idea of thinking about their painting or drawing before they start. Where do they want to put the tree? Is the car going to go by the tree or by the house? Space is particularly important in designing patterns. If you encourage the child to make patterns from geometric shapes or prints (see page 25) you are asking them to explore space in a formalised way. A pattern depends on the repetition of a shape or motif and the regularity of the spaces in between.

Although this particular goal links with art, craft, design and modelling, each element overlaps with other creative activities. Some older children may be ready to explore colour through mime and dance. How does the colour red make you feel? How can you express that feeling with your body? Colour also makes a good theme for poems based on similes - 'My jumper is as red as a strawberry/as red as an apple ...'

The word 'texture' can be applied to music as well as physical surfaces. Whenever the child listens to music, the combination of rhythm and melody gives her an experience of musical texture. 'Shape' and 'form' come into all creative activities. When the child makes up a story with a beginning, a middle and an end, she is giving it form. When she dances, she is creating shapes with her body. When she plays a simple tune or rhythm, she gives it a shape based on the notes and pattern of beats (see pages 34-37). 'Space' in the environment is explored through dance, role play, drama and mime, particularly where a partner or a group is involved. In music, spaces or 'rests' are as important to the tune as the beats, making up an integral part of the sound pattern.

When we look at colour, texture, shape, form and space in this way, it becomes clear how easy it is to satisfy this goal. Just about any creative activity or experience will be helping the child to explore these elements in one way or another.

## Helping the development of imagination

The Early Learning Goals state that, by the end of reception year, children should be able to 'use their imagination in art and design, music, dance, imaginative and role play and stories'. This is the goal that lists the areas of creative activity that we should be providing for the children:

❑ **art and craft** (drawing, painting, printing, collage, model making);

❑ **design** (pattern making, model making);

❑ **music** (singing, listening to music, playing instruments, beating rhythms with body movements and percussion);

❑ **dance** (including mime, music and movement and using the body to express ideas, feelings, and so on);

❑ **imaginative and role play** (drama related activities where the child takes on a role, using the imagination to develop it as far as she is capable);

❑ **stories** (creating a story or poem within a group or as an individual).

All of these activities demand a combination of imagination and practical or language skills with which to express creativity. Ultimately, the child needs to know how to handle a paint brush, mix colours and think about composition in order to express her imagination on paper - or how to beat out a rhythm, build up a pattern of sounds and use an instrument in order to create a piece of music. The creative activities that the child experiences throughout the Foundation Stage are important in helping the development of these skills. Having said that, the Foundation Stage is not just a preparation for later life. For the young child, the pleasure lies in the here and now, the process rather than the result. Any activities designed to help the child develop creative skills need to be enjoyable and absorbing.

It is also important to make space for the imagination to develop freely and naturally. Aim to balance activities that impart a skill with activities that are free and open-ended. For example, making clay tiles introduces the basic modelling skill of rolling and cutting clay, while using tools to decorate the tile enables each child to create her own individual piece.

Avoid activities that end up with ten identical pictures or models. One way of achieving this is to let the child do as much for herself as possible. A butterfly with wobbly wings cut out by the child is greatly preferable to a perfect butterfly cut out by you - and the child will have had a good opportunity to develop the fundamental skill of cutting. The same applies to music, drama, dance and storytelling. Always be ready to let the children take off in their own way. Creating music, drama or a group story will usually need some direction from you, but you should always allow the children to develop the activity within the structure you provide.

The most imaginative moments in the young child's life tend to occur spontaneously, during undirected time (see pages 18-19 for the role of play in Creative Development.) Making creative resources available to the children is important both in helping the development of imagination and as an emotional outlet.

Painting and drawing materials should always be accessible. With a little care and planning, musical instruments can also be put out for the children to use whenever they wish. Follow up a dance activity by creating a dance area with a tape recorder and tapes for the children to use. If free music and dance is disturbing to the group as a whole, try designating certain times of the day, or set up your music/dance area in a separate part of the setting.

As much as possible, discreetly observe the child's spontaneous use of creative resources. The chance to explore freely is essential but you can also step in with suggestions. Perhaps the two children playing with the piano could have the pedals pointed out to them, to give them new possibilities to explore. Perhaps the children who are playing the drum as they march about could be helped to build a marching rhythm into their activity. Ask a child to tell you about her painting or drawing, to encourage her to express her imagination in words.

You can also use your observations to help you plan appropriate activities. Aim to create a two-fold approach where the children are given both skills (an adult directed 'taught' activity) and the opportunity to use and develop their skills (child-centred exploration). For example, you may show your children how to use scissors and how to use glue, giving them cutting and gluing 'exercises' (see pages 26-29). You then need to let the children use their new skills of cutting and gluing with collage materials. As the children explore freely, look out for ways in which you can extend their skill. Offer them further directed activity, such as more advanced cutting exercises or showing them how to tear paper. Follow this up by giving the children more opportunities to explore the collage materials and consolidate their new skills.

Creating a supportive environment for the development of imagination is a three-fold task. Aim for:

❑ a good balance between activities that develop fundamental skills (cutting, using paint, beating out a rhythm, dance steps, performing in front of a group) and activities that are open-ended, allowing the children to express their imagination freely;

❑ creative resources (art and craft materials, musical instruments, role-play settings and props, dance tapes) made freely available and accessible to the children at all times;

❑ discreet observation of the children at play so that you can step in and give little pointers to further imaginative exploration. You can also use your observations as the basis for planning.

## Music

As we have seen, many of the Creative Development goals apply across a range of creative activities. One goal, however, is specifically related to music: 'recognise and explore how sounds can be changed, sing simple songs from memory, recognise repeated sounds and sound patterns and match movements to music'.

### Making and changing sounds

Babies can hear sounds up to three months before birth. From birth onwards, the child will be experiencing how she interacts with the world of sound, from eliciting a range of different sounds from her parents to creating sound when she throws her bricks across the floor or shakes her rattle.

Gradually, the child will come to realise that she herself can be the agent of making or changing sounds. The early years practitioner can build on this by helping her to create and explore a range of different sounds. Encourage the children to discover the different sounds they can make with everyday items - rattling keys, gently clinking a spoon against a plate, shutting the door, turning on the tap, swishing a thick paint brush across paper. Explore how you can make these sounds louder or softer before going on to look at different musical instruments. The opportunities for investigating how sound can be changed are endless, from striking different notes on the piano to pressing a finger on different parts of the guitar string or beating a drum hard or gently.

### Singing songs

Singing simple songs from memory is another skill that grows from babyhood onwards. This is where the older children in the setting can be a great help. Repeat simple songs that older ones already know and the little ones will gradually join in when they feel ready. Apart from being a pleasurable activity, the tune and the rhythm of a song make it easier for the child to remember the words. Add actions and movements to make positive use of fidgeting and help the children express ideas through movement.

### Sound patterns

Recognising repeated sounds and sound patterns is yet another skill that begins in babyhood. The baby babbles by repeating a syllable - ma-ma-ma - something that the adult will pick up on and repeat back to her. The much loved babyhood activity of throwing an object out of the cot again and again or shaking a rattle also give an experience of repeated sound. In the early years setting, you can build on this with simple clapping activities, songs and nursery rhymes with repeated refrains. As the children become ready, introduce more complex rhythms using different body percussion sounds and percussion instruments (see pages 35 and 42). This will help the child develop her ability to recognise sound patterns.

### Movement and music

Matching movement to music is a creative activity that involves the child recognising musical elements such as rhythm and pitch and interpreting the music in a way she can express with her body. Choose music with strong rhythms, distinct passages of high or low notes and a definite mood. Encourage older children to match a piece of music with something that falls within their realm of recent experience - weather, a familiar animal, a story character from a book you have just read. Moving to music does not have to express a specific object or experience. Show the children how to hop, skip, jump and move their arms in time to the music - the simplest form of dancing. As your children become ready, you can introduce a more complex dance by combining sequences of movement - six hops, six jumps, six skips, repeated as often as you wish. Encourage the children to develop their own dance routines. Circle dances make an easy formal dance for young children and there are plenty of old favourites to choose from - 'Ring o' Roses', 'In and Out the

Dusky Bluebells' or 'Here We Go Round the Mulberry Bush' (see pages 66-67 for more on circle dancing.)

## Creative expression

The final Creative Development goal is all about the ability to use a wide range of activities, tools and materials in order to express creativity. By the end of the Foundation Stage, the children should be able to 'express and communicate their ideas, thoughts and feelings by using a widening range of materials, suitable tools, imaginative and role play, movement, designing and making and a variety of songs and musical instruments'.

If the activities and experiences you plan for and encourage in your setting meet the other Early Learning Goals for Creative Development, they will automatically meet this one as well. If you sing, dance, play instruments, listen to music, paint, draw, model, cut and stick, mime, act, role play and create an environment where the children can play imaginatively, you will be laying invaluable foundations for creative expression. Once the child has gathered basic skills and experience with creative tools, materials and activities she can go on to choose whatever means she wishes to express her imagination.

Organise your setting so that a wide range of creative tools and materials are available for the children at all times. Provide a home corner, a dressing-up box, a dance area, a piano and percussion instruments, a painting easel and paints, supplies of drawing and painting paper, scissors, glue, materials for collage, Plasticene and playdough with cutters and tools. These are just some of the creative tools and materials that can be made constantly available to the children so that they can express themselves as and when they wish.

Something else you can do is to encourage the children to explore a theme or idea in many different ways. For example, you can paint cats, you can create stories and poems about cats, you can sing songs about cats, you can mimic cats using percussion instruments, you can make up a cat dance. Using a wide range of different creative approaches helps the children to develop a range of creative skills. It also offers something for everyone - movement and dance for the active child; language based activity for the verbal child; art and craft for the child who is adept with her hands; music and singing for the child with a good ear.

## Equal opportunities

Art, craft, music and dance make an accessible bridge into different cultures for young children. Show your group pictures and artefacts, listen to a range of music and introduce instruments from other countries. Diwali, Chinese New Year and Caribbean Carnival are all colourful festivals which can be used as a basis for art and craft activities. Wherever possible, invite artists, musicians and dancers into your setting to talk to the children and show them their art.

Creative activities also give free rein to the imagination so that you can become whatever you want. Boys and girls do not have to stick to traditional gender roles; this is the age at which it is easiest to encourage the children to be fluid in their creative play. Assign both caring and active drama, dance and mime roles to all children, regardless of gender or personality. Encourage everyone to enjoy and recreate nature in their art work, use modelling and construction toys, listen quietly to and appreciate music, dance, sing and express themselves in whatever way they wish.

The Early Learning Goals emphasise the importance of developing all the senses. This is particularly so for children with special needs. Activities that focus on touch, hearing and movement are valuable for children with sight or hearing impairments. Art, craft, modelling, dance and music can all be an alternative means of expression for the less verbal child or the child who does not have English as a first language. Creative expression can also be a therapeutic experience. Pummelling clay or stretching and jumping along to the music is a positive and constructive means of calming an unsettled child. While we must be careful about diagnosing emotional difficulties from children's art, it is worth remembering that creative activities provide an outlet, even for the youngest children.

## What to expect in music

Children vary enormously in their natural music abilities. Some children will arrive at your setting able to sing a tune and pick up a rhythm quite easily, while others may take much longer to develop these skills. By the time they move onto reception, most of your children should be able to listen to, assimilate and clap a simple, regular rhythm such as a nursery rhyme. They should also know how to get sound from a range of instruments and most should be able to distinguish between high/low and loud/quiet.

Shakers are the easiest percussion instruments to play. Start your youngest children with instruments such as rhythm eggs and maracas and move on to more challenging instruments as each child becomes ready. The easiest percussion for rhythm activities is a beating instrument - a drum or rhythm sticks. Make sure that children who find this activity difficult have access to these instruments.

Aim for your children to know a range of simple songs by the end of their pre-school years, although they will vary in their ability to hold a tune. During their time with you, most children will start to pick up the words of songs that are regularly repeated. This will include substituting their own versions for words they have misheard or putting in words that have a special meaning for them (the little boy who used his own surname by singing 'Baa Baa Blackshaw', for example). Most important of all, ensure that your children regard music and singing as pleasurable activities. This is far more valuable than being able to beat out a perfect 'Humpty Dumpty' with the maracas or sing 'Twinkle Twinkle' at the end-of-term concert.

## What to expect in art, craft and modelling

Your main aim with drawing and painting should be to let the children explore mark making - the so-called 'scribbling stage'. At around four years of age, most children will start to produce representational drawings. This means that the child has grasped the idea that a drawing can be of something, even if the subject of the drawing is not particularly recognisable.

As with music, the child's artistic abilities will vary enormously. Some children will start making representational drawings before the age of four and you may have the occasional child who produces such drawings at a much earlier age than the norm. This will depend on observational skills and hand-eye co-ordination. Such children often come from an artistic home where they have been exposed to art activities from a very early age.

By the time they leave your setting, most children should be able to distinguish and name common colours, as well as realise that new colours can be made through colour mixing. They should also be able to create models from a variety of materials and attempt simple modelling activities such as rolling a sausage and a ball from Plasticene or clay.

## What to expect in role play, dance and music and movement

The complexity of the child's imaginative and role play will develop along with her language skills and her group co-operation skills. Very young children tend to play in parallel rather than with other children, although the opportunity to watch other children at play is essential. Gradually, the child will join in more and more and you will see your older children starting to form the co-operative groups that are so characteristic of the next stage of development.

Very young children need realistic objects for pretend play - a toy tea set, model cars, miniature gardening tools. By the time they arrive in your setting, most children are becoming less dependent on realistic objects. The ability to pretend that an object represents something completely different will develop in the child throughout her time with you.

In planned role-play activities, even your youngest children should enjoy pretending to be something simple such as an animal, particularly if they are joining in with the rest of the group. As the child's understanding of story structure grows (the beginning, the ending, the main character), this will add to her ability to act out events and stories.

Children of all ages can join in circle dances and by the time they leave your setting, most children should be able to move in time to a rhythm and create a range of movements in response to music.

> Any suggestions as to what a child should be able to do must be regarded as flexible. While it is useful to have guidelines to help you plan appropriate activities for your group, it is important to remember that children vary in the pace at which they develop. The main aim of the early years worker should always be to observe, assess, value and cater for each child as an individual.

# Links with other areas of learning

The Early Learning Goals are divided into six areas of learning to help you plan across the curriculum. In practice, however, most activities satisfy a range of goals and few activities confine themselves totally to one area of learning. Many of the activities that fall within the Creative Development area will help the child develop a wide range of skills and capabilities.

Take as an example a group of children modelling with clay. As well as expressing themselves creatively, the children will be:

❑ maintaining concentration and working as part of a group through sharing tools (Personal, Social and Emotional Development);

❑ listening attentively as the adult explains the activity, and using language to organise, sequence and clarify their thoughts as the adult encourages the children to talk about what they are doing (Communication, Language and Literacy);

❑ exploring and using language to describe concepts such as 'more', 'less', 'greater', 'smaller', heavier' or 'lighter' as they play with the clay (Mathematical Development);

❑ investigating materials using the appropriate senses of sight, touch and smell (Knowledge and Understanding of the World);

❑ handling tools and malleable materials with increasing control as they mould the clay with their hands and cut, roll and decorate their models (Physical Development).

As part of your planning, it is always useful to scan through each activity in this way to check the range of goals you are covering. There are also some general links that can be made between Creative Development and the other five areas of learning.

## Personal, Social and Emotional Development

This is a wide ranging area of development, regarded as a pre-requisite for success in all other areas of learning. It includes the ability to understand and follow codes of behaviour, manage personal hygiene, show consideration for others and develop motivation for learning. The following aspects have a particular link with Creative Development.

### Group co-operation

Working harmoniously with others is a key aspect of Personal, Social and Emotional Development. Most adult directed art and craft activities take place in a group. Sharing glue, scissors, choosing materials, working quietly so as not to disturb others will all help your children towards group co-operation. Group singing, clapping rhythms, dance, role play and playing musical instruments also depend on working together. In order for a dance routine to work, each child needs to move in harmony with the other dancers. For a role play to be successful, each child needs to interact with the other children. Creative activities provide a range of different opportunities for the child to develop awareness of group co-operation and the ability to put that awareness into practice.

### Respect for other cultures

Art, craft, music and dance make an exciting and accessible means of introducing young children to different cultures. Festivals and celebrations such as Diwali or Chinese New Year provide opportunities for art and craft, music, dance and role play, particularly if you can invite visitors from other backgrounds into your setting. These experiences can make an important contribution to the development of tolerance and understanding. If young children discover the pleasure to be gained from other cultures, they are more likely to grow up with a respect for views and beliefs that differ from their own.

### Motivation to learn

All activities in the early years should be helping the children towards the goal of being interested and motivated to learn. Creative Development is a broad area. It offers something for everyone - from the energetic movement of dance to quiet, reflective moments at the painting easel. Music provides creative pursuits for the child with a good ear. Role play and story making is an outlet for the verbal child. Art, craft and model making suit the child with good hand-eye co-ordination and observation skills. And, more importantly, the variety of activities provides opportunities for every child in your setting to develop a rounded set of creative skills and abilities.

### Choosing activities and resources

Art and craft, music, singing, dance, imaginative and role play lend themselves particularly well to independent activity. They also introduce a wide range of different resources, tools and materials. Follow the pattern of showing the children how to use creative resources, giving them the opportunity to consolidate their new skills and then making the resources freely available in your setting. This will help the children develop the ability to select and use materials and resources independently.

## Communication, Language and Literacy

Language, literacy and communication skills are central to all aspects of a child's development. This area of learning covers the three broad elements of speaking and listening, reading and writing. Many aspects of Communication, Language and Literacy feed into Creative Development and vice versa - from playing with words to using the imagination to make up stories. The following aspects have a particular link with Creative Development:

### Language for learning

Most Creative Development activities encourage the children to use language in their play and learning. Explaining how to do something will help your group to develop listening skills. Encouraging them to talk about their pictures, dancing, singing and music will help them to develop speaking skills. For example, you can ask a child to tell you about the model she wants to make or the picture she intends to paint. Talk to the child about the musical instruments you are looking at or the dance you have just performed. Any creative group activity will also involve discussion and conversation, with opportunities for turn-taking, listening and the logical development of thoughts through spoken language.

### Words

Learning new words and exploring words and their sounds gives children a wide range of creative tools to use. Words are the building blocks of language and they are essential to any language based creative activity. Stories, poems, songs, rhymes, role play and imaginative play all depend on vocabulary and the child's realisation that she can explore and play with language. In their turn, creative activities and exploring with all the senses provide a great source of new vocabulary - from the texture words you might introduce through collage to the sound words that make up a part of your music activities.

### Drama and role play

Spoken language is central to any kind of drama. Role play, imaginative play and drama activities encourage the children to negotiate, plan and organise through language. They also provide a forum for the child to work towards the goals of 'us(ing) language to imagine and recreate roles and experiences and show awareness of the listener'. Many of these activities are performed before an audience. Communicating to the group as part of a performance is a special and unique way of showing awareness of your listeners.

### Stories, poems and the imagination

Imagination goes hand in hand with creativity, and language is perhaps the most immediate means of expressing the imagination. Many children will have listened to stories, poems, rhymes and songs from an early age. Gradually, they can start to express their own imaginative ideas through telling their own stories. The more stories and poems the children listen to, the better opportunity they have to absorb narrative structures, language patterns, rhythms and rhymes. The children can then draw on this experience as they develop their own story making skills (see pages 54-55).

### Preparation for reading and writing

Young children are laying foundations for the physical process of writing from the moment they start to make marks on paper. Early 'scribbles' with a pencil and free exploration with a paint brush help them develop the ability to hold and control a writing implement. Art, music and role play also make an early introduction to representation. Both reading and writing involve representing thoughts through symbols. In order to read and write for themselves, the children have to grasp the idea of symbols representing words, which in turn represent thoughts and ideas. When you encourage the children to draw a cat, or sing a song about a cat, or move like a cat, you are making an invaluable contribution to their discovery that one thing can represent or symbolise something quite different.

## Mathematical Development

Many mathematical concepts are most easily explored through creative activities. Music, dance, pattern, shape and form are just some of the activities and elements that are clearly mathematical as well as a part of the Creative Development area of learning. The following aspects have a particular link with Creative Development:

### Colour

Colour is a key element of art and craft. Through the creative exploration of colour, the child learns to recognise similarity, difference and even gradation (shade). Whenever the child chooses particular colours for her painting, she is using the mathematical skill of sorting - distinguishing between the red, the blue and the yellow and sorting one from the other. When she makes a red collage she is matching the red pieces with each other and sorting them from the other colours. For older ones, mixing paints or coloured chalks gives a new slant on the process of addition. If you add one colour to another you will end up with a different colour - an unusual opportunity for you to use the language of addition as part of a practical activity.

### Shape and form

Shape and form are important mathematical concepts, as well as being essential to creative activities. Perhaps the most obvious link lies with art and craft. Even the very youngest child will be exploring straight and curved lines, angles and shapes, whenever she draws. Collage paper pieces snipped into strips, triangles, rectangles and circles make a delightful way of introducing geometric shapes and enabling the children to explore their properties. Through painting, drawing and model making, the child will start to differentiate between two and three dimensions. There is no better way for a child to explore three-dimensional form than through manipulating and moulding clay, Plasticene or playdough for herself.

### Patterns

Making patterns involves organising motifs and spaces in ordered, regular ways. Drawing, painting, printing and decorating clay all help the child to explore, recognise and create patterns. Pattern is also to be found in music, songs, clapping games and dance routines. Counting the number of beats in a rhythm or creating a regular, repeated pattern of steps has a strong mathematical element, as well as providing the basis for music and dance.

### Mathematical qualities and language

Creative activities and the senses are essential to exploring mathematical concepts such as quantity, volume, weight and size. The hands-on nature of construction toys and modelling materials gives direct experience of weight and volume. Musical instruments may be large or small, heavy or light to hold. Dance involves number and position: 'Take three steps forward and three steps back', 'Stand in front of your partner', 'Stand beside your partner'. Look out for opportunities to introduce appropriate language as part of your spontaneous discussion with the children. For example, comment on how heavy the clay is, or how light the shaker is compared to the drum.

### Number

Number songs are one of the best ways of helping children learn to count through creative activities. Look out for songs with a role-play element such as 'Ten Green Bottles' or 'Five Little Speckled Frogs'. Use them to show the children how the quantity is made up and how it changes as each child joins or leaves the role-play group. Picture books are another useful creative resource when it comes to helping the child develop counting skills. Make good use of the words and pictures to show the children the different quantities (one butterfly, two birds, three sheep), listen to and join in with the words we use to count the quantities (one, two, three) and see how the symbols look in writing (1, 2, 3).

## Knowledge and Understanding of the World

This area of learning covers the child's exploration and discovery of her surroundings including people, objects, environmental qualities, the natural environment, science and technology, past events and different cultures and beliefs. The following aspects have a particular link with Creative Development:

### Using all the senses

The Creative Development goal 'respond in a variety of ways to what they see, hear, smell and touch' is closely linked with 'investigate objects and materials by using all of their senses as appropriate' from the Knowledge and Understanding of the World area of learning. The child uses a wide range of senses through creative activities: touch with model making, collage and playing musical instruments; hearing with songs, playing instruments and listening to music; sight through all the visual elements of art and watching carefully so that she can dance in time with the group or interact with her role-play partners. All of these activities play an important part in developing the senses so that the child is able to explore her surroundings fully.

### Similarities, differences, patterns and change

The ability to recognise these four elements is an important part of gathering knowledge and understanding of the world around you. The Early Learning Goal to 'look closely at similarities, differences, patterns and change' is a good example of a goal that stretches across several areas of learning - in this case Mathematical Development as well as Knowledge and Understanding of the World and Creative Development. We have already looked at similarity, difference and pattern in relation to maths. The fourth element, change, is a fundamental scientific concept and a part of many creative activities. Colour is changed when it is mixed with other colours; the sound of a musical instrument is changed when the child presses the string or bangs harder; her body shape changes whenever she moves her arms and legs as part of a dance. Creative activities are a constant exercise in discovering how great an effect a child can have when it comes to changing and shaping her surroundings.

### Construction tools and techniques

This is another aspect of Knowledge and Understanding of the World that links closely with Creative Development. Two of the goals require the children to 'build and construct with a wide range of objects' and 'select the tools and techniques they need to shape, assemble and join the materials they are using'. The creative activity of model making provides the main opportunity for working towards this goal in the early years setting. Cutting and sticking, making musical instruments, modelling with malleable materials and junk, cutting, rolling and decorating clay all make an important contribution to the child's ability to build, construct, shape, assemble and join.

### Other cultures

Finding out about other cultures is an important goal that we have already come across in the Personal, Social and Emotional Development list. Within the Knowledge and Understanding of the World area of learning, the emphasis is on people from other cultures as a part of the child's environment. Creative activities are a valuable means of introducing different cultures. Focus on using all the senses to explore different cultures - the colours, decoration and texture of clothes, the smell and taste of foods, the sounds of traditional music and song, the experience of exploring and playing instruments. Most young children are captivated by colour, detail, sound and texture. Exploring artefacts from other cultures provides a rich variety of sensory experiences as well as an introduction to different beliefs and ways of life.

## Physical Development

This area of learning covers all aspects of movement. Whereas the Creative Development goals focus on the expression of creativity and imagination, the Physical Development goals 'fill in' the practical and physical aspect of bringing creativity to fruition through the use of equipment, tools and malleable materials.

### Gross motor movements

These movements involve the large muscles of the body and include physical skills such as running, climbing, skipping and jumping. Dance and moving to music use many of these skills and require the children to direct, control and organise their movements in order to participate. Each child also needs to develop awareness of the space she and others are occupying - an important aspect of successfully taking part in a group role-play, dance or music and movement activity.

### Fine motor movements

Fine motor movement usually refers to any activity that involves hand-eye co-ordination. Most art and craft activities play an important role in developing fine movement: cutting with scissors, holding and wielding a pencil, controlling the amount of paint on a brush, manipulating a tiny collage piece to get it exactly where you want. Playing musical instruments also demands fine, controlled movements with the fingers and hands as you pluck the strings of a guitar or gently tap the chime bar. Many instruments can be played softly or loudly depending on how hard they are shaken, tapped or beaten. This involves quite a sophisticated degree of hand control.

### Using equipment

Equipment comes into most aspects of the child's experience in the early years setting. Scissors, gluing materials, paint brushes, pencils, crayons, objects for printing, musical instruments, tapes, tape recorders, dance, imaginative and role-play props and dressing-up clothes all have different qualities and purposes. Show each child how to use equipment and give her plenty of opportunity to consolidate her skills. As well as helping the children to express their imagination, this will also contribute to the development of overall hand-eye co-ordination.

### Using tools safely

The Physical Development goal 'handle tools, objects, construction and malleable materials safely and with increasing control' places emphasis on safety and control. Many art and craft materials need to be handled with care and many musical instruments, tapes and tape recorders, books and dressing-up clothes are delicate and have to be looked after. This is a two-fold process. The child needs to understand the concept of taking care and why this is important, and she needs to have the physical control to do so. Talk to the children about the reasons behind being careful, whether you want to protect a delicate object or ensure that no-one cuts themselves with the scissors. Remember that the ultimate responsibility always lies with the adult in the setting. Although the environment should be stimulating, it must also be safe - which includes not expecting more from your children than they can reasonably manage.

What Learning Looks Like...

**Creative Development**

# The importance of play

Play and creativity are closely linked. Regardless of whether the creative artist is a young child or an adult, many wonderful works of art can emerge from 'playing with' paint, clay, percussion instruments, dance steps or dressing-up clothes. But what exactly is play? And how can you tell the difference between play and work?

## Independent play

Play is commonly defined as something that children do spontaneously, without adult intervention and direction. While an activity doesn't stop being play if an adult joins in, many play occurrences in the early years setting will be child-centred. Observe your children during free, unstructured time and look out for some of the following, common (and valuable) features of play:

**Spontaneous activity, chosen by the child rather than adult directed**: for example, gathering leaves, twigs and stones in the garden and turning them into a pretend picnic or adapting and playing with the words, tune and rhythm of a familiar song.

**Consolidating and extending skills**: for example, playing with damp sand and using cutting and moulding skills learned during an adult directed session with playdough or clay.

**Open-endedness**: for example, role playing with the dressing-up clothes and creating scenarios that grow and develop spontaneously with no adult directed start or finish to the activity.

**Enjoying the process rather than the end result**: for example, building a tower of bricks and knocking them down or hopping, skipping and jumping up and down the slope in the garden, for no apparent purpose other than the sheer joy of the activity.

**The use of props**: for example, pretending to prepare a meal with a toy tea set, or turning an object such as a pencil holder into a completely unrelated object, such as a lorry.

**Exploring real life events**: for example, role playing bathing the baby; acting out a parent telling off a naughty child with puppets or dolls; playing 'police' or pretending to be a train driver.

Any one of these scenarios is likely to occur on a regular basis in the early years setting and each one is an example of valuable, spontaneous play with a particular link to creative activities.

## Play or exploration?

Many experts draw a distinction between play and exploration. Strictly speaking, much of what children do when left alone with art, craft or music resources would be classified as exploration rather than play.

In terms of providing your children with a stimulating setting, it does not really matter what you call activities. Play and exploration share many similar features and outcomes: discovery; the consolidation of skills; open-endedness; predominantly child-directed activity; taking pleasure in the process rather than putting emphasis on an end result. The important thing is to allow the children to engage in free and independent activity. As long as your environment is safe, carefully designed and well supervised, the children will do the rest when it comes to getting the most out of free play and exploration.

## Exploring art, music and dance

After you have introduced a creative activity, think through the ways in which you can make it freely available for the children to play with and explore. It is important to let the children consolidate and develop their skills with art, craft and modelling materials, musical instruments and dance. Try some of the following:

- ❑ Set up a drawing table where children can choose to sit and play with the pencils, wax crayons, chalks and paper (see page 20).

- ❑ Make the painting easel permanently available. Show the children the practicalities, such as how to put on an overall and how to clip on the paper and then leave them to explore freely (see page 62).

- ❑ An interactive music corner or display encourages children to explore and play with instruments and other music related activities (see page 44). Although you may have to restrict access to the percussion instruments and tape recorder (unless you provide headphones), aim to have some periods of the day when children are allowed to play freely with the instruments.

## An environment for imaginative and role play

Taking on roles and acting out fantasy situations are important activities for the young child. Imaginative and role play draw on language, communication and physical skills, helping the child to develop her understanding of the world and extend her imagination. They also give the child the opportunity to investigate situations that may be difficult, dangerous or uncomfortable. When a child pretends to be a firefighter or an angry parent, she is busy exploring a tricky event in the safety of the play situation, as well as enjoying herself.

Space, setting and opportunity are important in enabling the child to express herself through role and imaginative play. It is essential to build lots of play periods into your day and create an environment where children feel safe, comfortable and secure. Make sure that you have a well-equipped home corner; dressing-up clothes; play settings that reflect your current theme; a farmyard; a garage set; a dolls' house; a road mat with toy cars.

Choose imaginative and role-play props carefully. Provide a range of toys such as tea sets, household items, vehicles and gardening tools but also include neutral play items such as bricks, construction toys and modelling materials. Very young children need a realistic object in order to engage in pretend play. As children grow older, they become more able to invest an object with a different identity - a large leaf becomes a bowl, a collection of bricks becomes an aeroplane. This growing ability to use one thing to represent something completely different is an important part of creative play and something to be encouraged through providing a wide variety of non-representational playthings.

Apart from acting out domestic roles, young children tend to choose figures from television programmes or stories. Visits to outside places such as the zoo or the hospital can add inspiration to the child's role play, particularly if you follow up the visit by setting up a well-equipped role-play corner. Encourage the children to explore characters from picture books by providing appropriate story props. Figures made from card or fabric with Velcro loops on the back can easily be attached and removed from a felt board. Dressing-up clothes and props linked to a particular story will encourage the children to extend their story-based play and exploration. Start the children off by acting out the story together, using the clothes and props. These can then be made available for free play. If you choose a reality-based story such as Shirley Hughes' *Alfie* series, you can encourage older ones to think about what items from the story could be brought into the setting for play.

## Construction toys and materials

Construction toys make an invaluable resource in the early years setting because they have so many different uses. Their neutral nature means that they can be turned into whatever pretend play object the child wishes. They can also be used for constructing models, giving expression to the child's creative imagination. In the process, the child will make all kinds of scientific, technological and mathematical discoveries about elements such as balance, support, the properties of different structures and geometric shapes. Try to include basic, good quality wooden bricks, as well as some of the more sophisticated sets. Check that you have sets to suit the different ages and that units designed to be joined can be put together and taken apart easily.

## The role of the adult

While it is important that the child has the opportunity for independent play, there is no reason why adults shouldn't play, too. This can be a good way of introducing new ideas and extending the children's use of language and imagination. It can also encourage children who are reluctant to engage in role play. Research shows that imaginative play is less frequent amongst children who are not well acquainted with each other. If this is the case with your group, particularly at the start of the year, you can help by joining in.

Observe the children discreetly as they play. This can tell you a lot about their language and social capabilities and how they have taken on board the skills and knowledge you have offered, as well as how their artistic, musical and role-play skills are developing. Judge carefully when to step in with support - and when to leave the child to get on with whatever play activity she is engaged in.

When planning your creative activities, try to incorporate 'mini' opportunities for play. As much as possible, build in periods of free exploration.

All too soon, children start to distinguish between work and play. Creative activities are different from the other areas of the curriculum in that even adults regard them as play. With a little imagination, you can start the children off on a lifetime of creativity, with all the pleasure and enjoyment to be gained from art, drama, music and dance.

Creative Development

# Drawing

Drawing is central to all art and craft activities and important in helping the children develop fine motor movements. There are many different drawing implements that can be used by even your youngest children. For example, pencils of all grades (H, HB, B, 2B), coloured pencils, wax crayons, coloured chalks, pastels, charcoal and felt pens. These activities start off with the basic skills of drawing for the very youngest children. There are also activities for older children, showing some simple drawing techniques and effects that can be created with different mark making implements.

## Using the drawing table

Introduce drawing materials to the child as soon as possible after she joins your group. Once she knows where to find the drawing things and how to use them, she can draw freely whenever she wishes.

**Early Learning Goals**

These activities will help you work towards the following goals:

❑ Explore colour, shape, texture, form and space in two dimensions.

❑ Express and communicate ideas, thoughts and feelings by using a widening range of materials and suitable tools.

❑ Use imagination in art and design.

❑ Respond in a variety of ways to what they see, touch and feel.

This activity links with the following Stepping Stones:

❑ Differentiate marks and movements on paper.

❑ Use lines to enclose a space, then begin to use these shapes to represent objects.

❑ Make ... drawings.

❑ Work creatively on a large or small scale.

❑ Respond to comments and questions, entering into dialogue about their creations.

### What you will need

Pencils; a supply of paper; a large table and chairs in a corner of the setting, designated 'the drawing table'.

### Getting ready

Gather a selection of pencils with a variety of grades, including some in chubby sizes. H is hard, HB is the standard writing grade, B and 2B are drawing pencils, creating a softer, smudgier effect. Place the pencils in an attractive pencil pot. Cut some sheets of paper, providing a range of sizes and colours and including white cartridge paper if your budget will allow. Set up a special table where the children can sit and draw. Display the pencils, paper and other drawing materials in the middle of the table.

### What to do

Show the children the drawing table with the pencils, paper and so on. Explain that they can sit and draw at the table whenever they choose. Remind them to ask for their names to be written on their drawings.

Leave little ones to explore freely with the drawing implements.

Keep an eye on how older children are holding the pencil. If a child is progressing well with pencil control, the grip does not matter. If her way of holding the pencil seems to be hampering her, you could gently encourage her to try a more traditional grip.

If you have a spare moment, sit down at the drawing table to do your own drawing. This is a good way of modelling an effective pencil grip as well as sparking interest in the activity. Persuade helpers to do likewise; if they are anxious about their drawing skills, reassure them that young children are not judgemental about other people's art work!

Don't worry if the children seem to be producing nothing but 'scribble'. This is the only way for them to become familiar and comfortable with a pencil. Observe them drawing. As their lines become more controlled and they start to produce enclosed shapes, try introducing one or two of the activities below.

## Using different drawing materials

The following activities offer some suggestions for exploring different drawing materials and the effects that can be created. Use them as a 'pick and mix', choosing techniques to suit

different ages and levels of ability.

Once you have introduced a new drawing implement, such as the coloured chalks, add them to your drawing table (see above) to enable the children to explore and consolidate the skills you have shown them. Keep an eye on free use of the messier materials such as chalks and charcoal. Make sure that overalls are worn and hands washed.

These activities link with the same Stepping Stones as 'Using the drawing table' plus:

❑ Begin to differentiate colours/ Explore what happens when they mix colours (coloured pencils, wax, chalks).

❑ Experiment to create different textures.

## Pencils

You will need paper and pencils of various grades. Show the children the following techniques:

❑ Pressing hard/softly with the pencil to create light and dark shades (works best with a B or 2B pencil).

❑ Drawing zig-zags, short lines or dots to create different patterns and textures in a drawing.

❑ Smudging pencil lines and shaded areas with a finger to create a misty effect (works best with a B or 2B pencil).

❑ Using the length of the pencil point to create a thick, shaded line. Choose a B or 2B pencil and make sure that it is well sharpened. This technique is quite challenging, as you have to get the angle of the pencil just right. Save it for older children with good hand control.

## Wax crayons

You will need good quality wax crayons and coloured sugar paper. Washable crayons are good for getting off clothes but they are not the best choice for art work! Show the children the following techniques:

❑ Pressing hard/softly with the crayon to create light and dark shades.

❑ Drawing zig-zags, short lines, crosses or dots to create patterns and different textures in a drawing.

❑ Using different parts of the crayon to produce a range of effects, such as the whole length of the crayon to create a shaded area or the round flat end to produce circles.

❑ Mixing colours by crayoning one on top of another. Always use the darker one first, such as blue before yellow. Show the children how to press lightly with the blue and hard with the yellow.

❑ Colour thick layers of wax onto a card and then indent patterns into the wax with a pencil. Try rubbing a layer of black over the other colours or painting thick black paint over the wax to make a scratch card.

❑ Draw pictures with wax crayons and then wash over with a thin paint solution to make wax resist pictures.

## Coloured chalks

You will need good quality chalks in different colours, including white; a range of different coloured paper, including black or dark blue. Chalk is a wonderfully messy medium. Wear painting overalls and wash hands after use. Show the children the following techniques:

ACTIVITY

❑ Many of the pencil and wax crayon techniques can also be used with chalk. Try pressing hard and lightly; drawing zig-zags, lines, crosses and dots; shading with the length of the chalk; putting one colour on top of another.

❑ The special quality of chalk is its smudginess. Show the children how to smudge chalk lines and dots with a finger (see 'Making firework pictures' for more ideas).

### Coloured pencils

You will need good quality coloured pencils, including some chubby shapes for younger children and white cartridge paper. Show the children the following techniques:

❑ All the pencil drawing techniques can also be used with coloured pencils. Try pressing hard and lightly; making zig-zags, lines, crosses and dots; shading with the length of the pencil point.

❑ Show older children how to colour in an area of paper. Draw an outline and use zig-zags, working across the shape in strips.

❑ Mix colours by shading one area of colour on top of another. Always use the darker colour first and press harder with the lighter colour.

### Charcoal

You will need charcoal and cartridge or sugar paper. Try using different thicknesses of charcoal if you are able to buy a mixed box. Use the same techniques as for pencils and make the most of the smudgy quality of charcoal. Use with older ones and show them how to grip the charcoal stick near the point so that it doesn't break. Like chalk, charcoal is messy. Wear painting overalls and wash hands after use.

## Making firework pictures

This activity uses the special qualities of chalk on black paper to create the effect of fireworks.

It links with the following Stepping Stones:

❑ Begin to differentiate colours/ Explore what happens when they mix colours/Choose particular colours to use for a purpose.

### What you need

Coloured chalk; black sugar paper; cotton wool balls; painting overalls.

### Getting ready

Cut your sugar paper into A4 sized pieces - you do not need large sheets for this activity.

### What to do

Start off by talking about Bonfire Night and the different fireworks - their names, the sounds they make and, in particular, their colours. You can then show the children how to smudge chalk marks to create a bright, fluorescent firework effect on the black paper.

Younger ones can simply concentrate on making marks with different coloured chalk and then rubbing them. If they are not keen on using fingers (or you want to minimise mess) give them cotton wool balls. You can also take the opportunity to use the colour names as much as possible to help them distinguish and identify the different colours.

Older ones can try a number of more refined techniques. Try smudging different shaped marks - dots, lines, criss-crosses. A heavy dot which is then smudged to one side creates a tail like a rocket shooting across the sky. A circle of chalk can be smudged round and round to create a halo of light like a Catherine wheel. Try smudging a shower of dots to represent little stars or sparklers. Try chalking one colour on top of the other and then rubbing them together. Encourage the children to think about which colours to use for particular fireworks.

As with all art work, give the children techniques and ideas and then leave them free to create their own individual pieces.

## Drawing plants

This activity introduces observational drawing - looking closely at an object and then drawing what you see. It is an activity for older children although you may occasionally have younger children in your group who are ready. If a child is starting to identify her drawings, she is on the way to being ready for observational drawing. When she tells you that she has drawn a cat, a house, or a car (even if it is not recognisable to you), she is demonstrating that she has grasped the concept of drawing as representational.

Leaves, flowers and plants make suitable objects for drawing. They are easily accessible and they offer interesting colours and shapes ranging from simple to complex. If you choose objects from nature, you could link this activity with the 'Seasons' theme.

The activity contributes to the same Stepping Stones as 'Using the drawing table' plus:

❑ Begin to use representation as a means of communication.

### What you will need

Pencils; coloured pencils; paper in natural and neutral shades; a selection of leaves, flowers and plants.

### Getting ready

Gather leaves, flowers and plants. Group them into simple, medium and complex according to shape. Leaves and flowers can be easier to draw and will last longer if you press them first. Use a custom-made flower press or place them between sheets of tissue in an old telephone directory, with piles of heavy books on top. The leaves should press within a week - particularly dry autumn leaves. Thick, fleshy flowers will take longer. Protect them by slipping them into clear plastic folders.

### What to do

Select some leaves with simple shapes and look at them closely. Point out the outline and the pattern of veins on the leaf. Use a magnifying glass to encourage close observation. Show the children how to draw a picture of the leaf on the paper, emphasising that you are looking very closely and drawing what you see.

Don't expect exact drawings. The children will tend to draw what they know about a leaf rather than what they can actually see. The aim of this activity is to encourage observation and introduce the idea of observational drawing, rather than produce an exact copy of the object.

As the children become ready, introduce leaves, flowers and plants with more complex shapes. They can also use the coloured pencils and start to think about which colour paper they want to use.

If you feel your group would respond better to drawing different objects, choose whatever would suit their interests. As with leaves and flowers, start off with simple shapes, progressing to something more complex as the children become ready.

## Other activities

Once the children have grasped the idea of looking at something and drawing what they see, encourage them to wander around the setting and garden finding other objects to draw. They can either sit down with a clipboard or bring a portable object to the table.

Use the smudged chalk technique for any picture that involves lights - Christmas lights, seaside illuminations, Diwali, a starry sky.

Link drawing with the Stepping Stone 'Understand that different media can be combined' by encouraging the children to mix drawing materials. Make all the drawing materials available and let the children use chalks, wax crayons and coloured pencils within the same drawing.

### Assessment

❑ Drawing provides good opportunities for you to observe whether or not the child is gripping the pencil adequately. Look out also for how well the child controls the pencil in mark making, enclosing spaces with lines and, later, creating representational drawings.

❑ Record the point at which each child starts to make representational drawings. The usual age range for this to occur is between 3.5 to 4.00 onwards. Look out for understanding rather than recognisable images.

❑ People tend to be amongst the earliest representative drawings in the child's repertoire. Watch how the detail develops, starting with a large head, eyes and mouth and progressing to hair, bodies and limbs. Some children may be adding fingers, toes and more refined facial details by the time they leave your setting.

❑ Observe how well the children absorb the different drawing techniques you show them. Many involve controlling lightness or firmness of touch. This is a good indicator of how fine motor movements are progressing overall.

❑ Look out for whether the older child selects different media and colour of paper. Does she combine media such as pencil, wax and chalk within the same picture?

❑ Try to gather a selection of significant drawings with name and date on the back as a record of how the child's skills are progressing. This will give you a much better overview of the child's progress than taking 'snapshot' sample drawings at set times throughout the year.

# Printing

Printing is one of the best ways of introducing pattern to the young child. Each printed image is the same as the last so the child can concentrate on organising motifs and spaces to create her pattern. Before she reaches this stage, the child needs to develop printing skills and in the early stages she should be left simply to explore, experiment and enjoy printing. Printing is yet another art activity that helps to develop co-ordinated and controlled hand movements, as well as offering new creative possibilities.

## The beginnings of printing

This activity introduces printing and highlights the challenges the child needs to overcome to print successfully.

The activity links with the following Stepping Stones:

❑ Differentiate marks and movements on paper.

❑ Work creatively on a small and large scale.

### What you will need

Ready-mixed liquid paint; sponge circles in saucers; paint pots and brushes; sugar paper; newspaper; objects to print with.

### Getting ready

There are two ways of covering an object with paint ready for printing:

❑ painting the object with a paint brush;

❑ pressing the object onto a paint-soaked sponge pad.

Choose the technique that best suits the object you are using. For example, a carrot can be pressed into a sponge pad whereas a hand is more easily painted. Visit a local furniture upholsterer and ask for thin sponge off-cuts to cut into circles. Soak the circles in water and then squeeze out the excess so that the sponges are damp. Put a blob of ready-mixed paint onto the centre of the circle. Unless your paint is very thick, you do not need to water it down if the sponge is moist.

Provide just a couple of colours to begin with and a simple object that is easy for the child to hold. Cotton reels, pieces of sponge or half a carrot are all good for beginners. Make sure you have spare newspaper or scrap paper handy for first attempts.

Choose a colour of sugar paper that contrasts with your paint. You can use any paper to print on but sugar paper works particularly well because it has a slightly absorbent surface.

### What to do

There are four main challenges to printing:

❑ Getting a firm, comfortable grip on your object;

❑ Covering the whole surface of the printing object with paint;

❑ Holding the object still on the paper when you press down;

❑ Holding the paper still with your hand as you lift off the object.

Show the children how to make a print, emphasising these four challenges. Let them explore and enjoy the printing, introducing one or two more objects if you want to show them some different prints. If the printing object becomes clogged with paint, show how to blot off the excess on scrap paper or newspaper.

Look at the results with the children and point out the difference between the first prints and the later prints as the paint becomes used up.

> **Early Learning Goals**
>
> These activities will help you work towards the following goals:
>
> ❑ Explore colour, shape, texture, form and space in two dimensions.
>
> ❑ Express and communicate ideas, thoughts and feelings by using a widening range of materials and suitable tools.
>
> ❑ Use imagination in art and design.
>
> ❑ Respond in a variety of ways to what they see, touch and feel.

## Printing with different objects

There is a huge range of different objects that you can print with. Try some of the following:

❑ sponge pieces and shapes (cut upholsterer's off-cuts into shapes using an electric carving knife);

❑ carrots and potatoes cut in half;

❑ dried beans or rice and circles of muslin tied into bundles;

❑ any object glued onto a block of wood, such as a key, paper-clip, hair grip;

❑ cotton reels;

❑ string, pasta or cut-out card shapes glued onto a block of wood (older children can make their own);

❑ leaves with strong vein patterns and long stalks for holding onto;

❑ half a lemon, orange, apple, mushroom, broccoli or cauliflower (leave juicy fruits to dry out first);

❑ hand, finger and footprints (make sure you have a source of water nearby for washing).

Choose objects that are easy for younger ones to hold - sponges, carrots and potatoes, bean bundles, objects glued onto wood blocks, cotton reels. Limit the number of objects and paints. Although you are introducing the children to printing, some little ones will paint rather than print with their object. This probably means they are not yet ready to grasp the concept or purpose of printing. Leave them to explore and enjoy the materials in their own way and re-introduce printing when they are a little older. As a preparation, you can show them how to press Lego, Stickle bricks and other patterned objects into playdough.

Challenge older ones to keep their object still on the paper so that they get the clearest print possible. If they are ready, help them to make their own printing objects such as string and card blocks. Introduce a range of paints, objects and different coloured sugar paper and encourage the children to choose their own materials.

## Printing patterns

This activity gives the children a simple, easy-to-use technique for creating a pattern. At the same time, the children can be encouraged to use their imaginations by picking their own combinations of printing objects and colours.

The activity links with the same Stepping Stones as 'The beginnings of printing', plus:

❑ Use ideas involving fitting, overlapping, in, out, enclosure, grids and sun-like shapes;

❑ Choose particular colours to use for a purpose.

### What you need

Sugar paper; pencil and ruler; sponge paint pads or paint pots and brushes; objects for printing.

### Getting ready

Prepare paint pads and printing objects (see 'The beginnings of printing' and 'Printing with different objects').

Rule lines and grids onto sheets of sugar paper. Create as many variations as you wish: horizontal and vertical lines, grids, large and small squares, diagonal lines, circles.

### What to do

Show the children how to print within the pattern of lines on the paper. Start off with the simplest pattern of straight horizontal lines and help the child to print along the line. Let each child choose her own printing object but make sure that she is familiar with all the objects you provide for this activity.

Observe how each child is managing this activity and offer more complex grids as he or she becomes ready.

Younger children will still be developing their printing skills. Some may be ready to try a simple pattern of straight horizontal lines but keep the emphasis on free exploration.

Older children can be encouraged to think about the colours they choose, and the combination of objects. For example, what object would work well printed within a line of circles? What two objects and colours would look good in a grid of small and large squares?

Once the paint has dried, the guidelines can be rubbed out and the print used for mounts, wrapping paper, folders, book covers or wallpaper for dolls' houses.

**Assessment**

❑ Do your younger children understand the concept of printing? If a child tends to paint rather than print with the object, she is probably not yet ready for the activity.

❑ Observe the children to see how well they can control their hand movements as they lower the object onto the paper, keep it still and hold the paper down when lifting the object up again.

❑ Are your older children able to create a pattern? Placing the printing object within the squares, lines or circles of the grid involves quite a degree of hand control. How successful are they, and how creatively can they choose and combine different objects and colours?

**Creative Development**

# Collage

Collage is a versatile activity that uses a number of art and craft based skills. The word collage comes from the French *coller* meaning 'to stick'. Stick whatever you like onto a background and you will end up with a collage picture.

Cutting and sticking are fundamental to collage. Once the children have mastered sticking, they can make collage pictures using objects or ready cut shapes. Once they have started to cut, they can create their own shapes for collage. There is a huge variety of materials, papers and objects that can be used for collage (see 'All kinds of everything' below). The materials and objects provide texture, colour and shape so that even the simplest picture made by the youngest child looks effective. Older ones can be encouraged to think about composition. Unlike painting or drawing, collage pieces can be arranged and re-arranged until you have them just as you want before sticking them down. This enables your older ones to think about and experiment with composition, design and the relationship between space and detail in a picture.

These activities include two planned projects: bean and pasta plaques and Chinese New Year dragons. Both projects are designed to give the children a structure within which they can create their own, individual work. The projects can also be adapted to suit different ages.

## Cutting cards

These simple cutting cards are useful for practising the skill of cutting. Cutting up to the horizontal line keeps the cutting card complete so that it can be stored as a record of the child's progress. It also provides an added challenge - knowing when to stop is an important aspect of cutting! The cards are graded in difficulty: straight lines, wavy lines and zig-zags.

### What you will need

Cutting cards (see illustration below); blunt-ended scissors.

### Getting ready

Prepare cutting cards: cut thin card into A5 size. Rule a black felt-pen line horizontally across the top, about 3 cm from the edge. Rule straight vertical lines from the bottom of the card to the line (see below). If you have older children, make some more advanced cards with wavy and zig-zag lines. Thin card is the easiest material for young children to cut.

### What to do

Show the children how to hold the scissors and cut along the straight lines of their cutting card. Show them how to stop at the horizontal line.

Let the child cut as many cards as she wishes. As she becomes ready, you can introduce cards with wavy lines and zig-zags. Zig-zags are the most challenging because the child keeps on having to change direction.

If you have some enthusiastic cutters, provide them with strips of coloured paper and card to cut into pieces. The different colours can then be saved in

**Early Learning Goals**

These activities will help you work towards the following goals:

- ❑ Explore colour, shape, texture, form and space in two dimensions.
- ❑ Express and communicate ideas, thoughts and feelings by using a widening range of materials and suitable tools.
- ❑ Use imagination in art and design.
- ❑ Respond in a variety of ways to what they see, touch and feel.

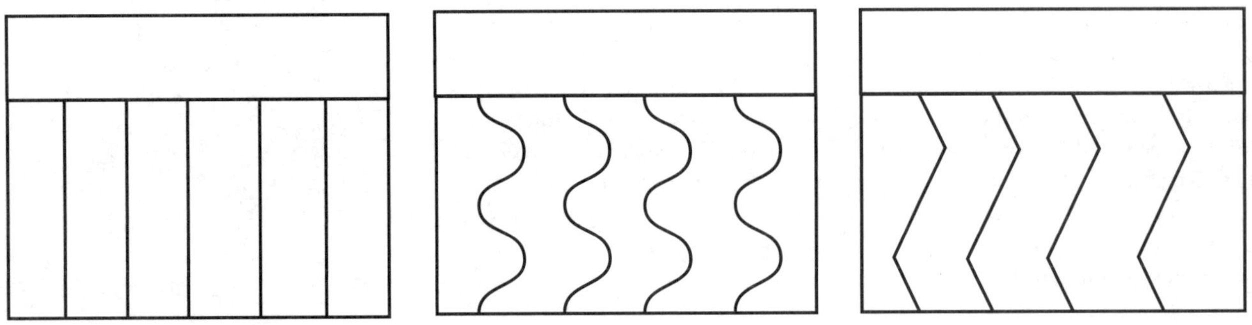

yoghurt pots for making collage mosaics.

You can also give the children geometric and other shapes drawn onto paper or card. If you cut roughly around the shape first, it is much easier for the child to cut out than working with a large, unwieldy piece of paper.

## Extension ideas

Some children with good hand control may be ready to try tearing paper for collage. Although it is easy to tear randomly, it is difficult to do so with control. Give the children 'tearing cards', made from thin, tearable paper and following the same pattern as cutting cards. See how well they can manage to tear along the lines, curves and zig-zags and encourage them to tear shapes for their free collage.

## Sticking

The aim of this activity is to introduce, focus on and practise the skill of sticking.

### What you will need

Glue and spatula or brush; small pieces of paper or flat objects for sticking; backing paper to stick onto; sheets of thin paper such as typing paper.

### What to do

Vary your approach depending on the age group you are working with:

❑ Younger children find it much easier to put a blob of glue on the backing paper and then place whatever they are sticking on top of the glue, rather than putting the glue onto the object to be stuck. Encourage them not to use too much glue. If you are using a spatula or brush, show them how to wipe off the excess on the edge of the pot.

❑ Some older children with lots of sticking experience and good hand control can try spreading glue on the back of whatever they are sticking. Show them how to put glue right to the edge - but only a tiny amount or it will squelch out from underneath. When they have turned their shape over and put it on the backing paper, show them how to place a sheet of thin paper on top and smooth across it with one hand. This presses out any wrinkles.

## Collage pictures

Cutting and sticking skills are not an end in themselves. The whole point of being able to cut and stick is to use your skills to make wonderful collage pictures.

This activity links with the following Stepping Stones:

❑ Use ideas involving filling, overlapping...

❑ Experiment to create different textures.

❑ Work creatively on a small or large scale.

❑ Choose particular colours to use for a purpose.

❑ Show an interest in what they touch and feel/Further explore an experience using a range of senses.

### What you will need

Glue; scissors (depending on the materials you use); background paper; objects, materials or papers for collage (see 'All kinds of everything' below).

### What to do

Begin by introducing a small group of children to just one or two materials, for example, wallpaper and felt shapes. Show them how to arrange and stick the pieces on background paper to create a collage picture.

Continue to introduce materials in this way until the children are familiar with a range of collage substances and have had several opportunities to make collage pictures. Although it can be tempting, try to avoid overwhelming the children by giving them everything all at once.

At this point, you can put out the scissors, the glue, the backing paper and a selection of different things so that a child can choose to make a collage as an independent activity - just as she would choose to go and draw or paint at the easel.

Leave the children free to use the collage materials in their own individual way, changing and adding substances to maintain interest.

Let younger ones explore the materials and develop their sticking and cutting skills through collage. Give them simple materials to use, such as ready-cut wallpaper pieces, large, strong pressed leaves and felt shapes.

Extend the activity for older ones by showing them how to make a background for their collage, using one or two rectangles or overlapping shapes and strips stuck onto the backing paper. Making a background gives the children a new technique and adds unity to the picture. Talk to the children about choosing contrasting colours - pale muted colours for the background and bright colours and shapes that will stand out for the foreground. You can also show the children how to arrange and rearrange their details to get them just as they want before the final sticking.

## All kinds of everything

The following make up just some of the many materials you can use for collage:

❑ Recycle scraps of card and sugar paper from other activities and talk to the children about the importance of re-using paper; keep wallpaper off-cuts, old wrapping paper and brown paper. Even newspaper can add interesting patterns and textures to a picture.

❑ Silver foil can be crumpled up or left smooth. Compare the matt surface on one side and the shiny surface on the other. Try drawing patterns onto one side and turning over to see the raised lines, or stick an object with a distinctive shape onto card and then press silver foil on top.

❑ Tissue paper is a wonderful resource for collage. It can be difficult to handle, so you may prefer to save it for older children. Try tearing it, crumpling it into little balls, scrunching it up and then smoothing it out to create interesting textures, placing several layers on top of each other to make a richer colour. Don't worry about blobs of glue showing through - this adds to the effect.

❑ Look out for substances with contrasting textures. Sandpaper, cotton wool, pieces of velvet, dried flowers and glossy paper all have interesting textures. Sandpaper is too tough for the children to cut for themselves - cut it into shapes for them to use. Choose substances to represent a range of textures: smooth, rough, bumpy, fluffy and so on. Show the children how to make collage pictures using separate pieces of paper for each texture. Stick them to the wall side by side like tiles to make a feely mosaic. Encourage the children to feel and name the substances and textures.

❑ Sprinkly things such as glitter, sand and dried lavender are all lovely for older ones although you need to give a little thought to the technique you use. Try putting the glitter or sand in a salt shaker so that it can be sprinkled onto the glue. Another technique is to pick up glitter between index finger and thumb. This limits the amount of glitter sprinkled onto the picture, although you need to watch out for children rubbing their eyes with glittery fingers. A third approach is to spread the glitter or sand on a tray and show the children how to lay the paper on the glitter, glue side down.

❑ Pressed flowers and leaves make beautiful collages, particularly if you choose the colour of background paper to set off their colours. You can also use twigs, small pebbles, shells, seeds, sheep's wool and other natural objects. This makes a lovely focus for a nature walk - although do check that nothing poisonous is collected. Freshly collected rose petals look beautiful against brilliant white card, and you end up with a collage that changes day by day as the petals gradually dry out.

❑ Fabrics make colourful collage pictures and you can introduce a variety of different colours and textures. Younger ones can use ready-cut pieces. Older ones can cut out their own shapes but you may need to select the fabrics carefully as some are not easy to cut. If older ones want to draw shapes first, give them white chalk. Provide card as a background, rather than paper - it is better able to take the weight of the fabrics.

❑ String, wool and embroidery threads offer a range of interesting colours and textures. Put the glue onto the paper and lay the string on top rather than attempting to glue the string itself. Save these materials for older ones and be ready to give a little help.

## Bean and pasta plaques

Pressing beans and pasta into rolled out Plasticene is collage without the cutting and sticking. This means that even the very youngest children can make their own plaque, with little help from you. The activity also enables the children to create pictures from the wonderful array of dried beans available, without the accompanying difficulties of sticking small, curved shapes onto paper.

The activity links with the same Stepping Stones as 'Collage pictures', also:

❑ Understanding that different media can be combined.

### What you will need

Plasticene; card; scissors; a sharp knife or biscuit cutters; a selection of pasta shapes and dried beans in small, separate containers; PVA glue; high gloss wood or craft varnish; thin ribbon.

### Getting ready

Roll out the Plasticene, leaving it thick

enough to hold the beans and pasta. Cut the Plasticene into circles, squares and diamonds and glue each plaque onto a piece of card cut to the same shape.

Gather together your dried beans and pasta shapes, choosing a range of colours and shapes such as small, dark green mung beans, black eyed beans, yellow split peas, small, red aduki beans, pale green flageolet beans. Avoid red kidney beans as they can be toxic when uncooked. Place the beans and pasta in separate containers.

### What to do

Show the children how to press beans into the Plasticene to make patterns.

❑ Leave younger ones to enjoy the experience of manipulating the beans and pressing them into the Plasticene to make a random pattern.

❑ Older ones can also be left to create their own random patterns or you can show them how to press a bean into the centre of the plaque and then work around it, building up rings of different colours and shapes.

When the plaques are finished you can varnish them with high gloss varnish (once the children have gone home.) The varnish brings out the colours of the beans and makes them glow, as well as ensuring that nothing falls out of the Plasticene. Attach a loop of ribbon to the back so that the plaque can be hung on the wall and you have the perfect hand-made present for Mother's Day or Christmas.

## Chinese New Year dragons

Collage is useful for festive art and craft because there are so many brightly coloured papers and shiny, sparkly bits and pieces to choose from. Link this activity with the Chinese New Year (January/February).

This activity contributes to the same Stepping Stones as 'Collage pictures'.

### What you will need

Festive papers and collage materials such as crepe and tissue paper, shiny gold and silver paper, ribbons, large sequins, tinsel and glitter; lolly sticks; paper fasteners; stiff green card; pencil; scissors; glue.

### Getting ready

Cut out a dragon's head and two or three body sections from green card, one for each child (copy or trace and enlarge the picture.)

Prepare the coloured papers: either cut them into streamers or divide them into smaller pieces so that the children can cut out their own. Make sure that you have plenty of orange, red and yellow for the dragon's fiery breath. If you have a mixed bag of sequins, sort out the large ones and place them in a container.

Gather your lolly sticks. Either plan in advance and collect used ones or buy from your art supplier (they will probably be called craft sticks or tongue depressers.)

### What to do

Show the children how to glue shapes and streamers onto the dragon's head and body. Crumple up red, yellow and orange tissue for its fiery breath. Stick on large sequins for its eyes. Encourage the children to use a wide range of bright colours to make it as eye-catching as possible.

Younger ones can use ready-cut shapes and streamers.

Older ones can cut and tear their own shapes and streamers. You can also introduce glitter and some different ways of using tissue paper (see 'All kinds of everything').

Once the children have decorated their head and body parts, the dragon can be assembled. Attach the pieces at each end with gold paper fasteners. The children can help you with this part of the activity but do supervise carefully. A lolly stick can then be glued to the back of each section. The resulting dragon has a flexible body that can be manipulated by moving the lolly sticks up and down.

### Assessment

❑ Keep cutting cards for each child with the name and date on the back, as a record of the child's progress. These will only give you a partial assessment, however. Look out also for how the child handles scissors during collage work.

❑ How well can the children control a glue spatula or brush? Do they understand the need for the right amount of glue?

❑ Observe how creatively the children make their collage pictures and whether older ones are starting to experiment with the arrangement of pieces (composition) before sticking. Are they able to choose contrasting colours to make the background and the foreground?

❑ Once you have set up a collage table, observe how independently the children can choose their materials, cut, stick and make their pictures. Do they understand the need to tidy up after themselves and leave the table ready for the next person?

# Modelling

With the possible exception of finger painting, modelling is the most hands-on of the art and craft activities. Getting hands dirty with clay or building structures from junk is wonderfully therapeutic for young children - and full of creative possibilities.

Modelling is an important means of introducing three-dimensional form to the child because the child can create and change the forms for herself. Modelling activities also give new opportunities to explore thoughts and ideas through artwork, as well as using a range of art related skills - cutting, sticking, decorating models with paint and other media and creating patterns in the surface of damp clay.

There are many modelling materials on the market. Do experiment with them if your budget allows, but most possibilities can be covered with playdough and clay.

## Exploring playdough

The soft consistency of playdough makes it the easiest modelling material for little ones to use. As with all art and craft materials, the first step is to show the children the practicalities and then leave them to get on with exploring the playdough in whatever way they wish. Provide tools and show the children a few techniques, but give them plenty of space to exercise their imaginations. Playdough is a good material for encouraging children to make representative objects because it is so malleable and easy to use. Watch your children as their play develops from squeezing, pulling and stretching the playdough to making 'sandwiches', 'cakes' or 'vehicles'.

**Early Learning Goals**

These activities will help you work towards the following goals:

❑ Explore colour, shape, texture, form and space in two dimensions.

❑ Express and communicate ideas, thoughts and feelings by using a widening range of materials and suitable tools.

❑ Use imagination in art and design.

❑ Respond in a variety of ways to what they see, touch and feel.

This activity links with the following Stepping Stones:

❑ Make three-dimensional structures.

❑ Experiment to create different textures.

❑ Work creatively on a small or large scale.

❑ Show an interest in what they touch and feel/Further explore an experience using a range of senses.

❑ Use one object to represent another, even when the objects have few characteristics in common.

❑ Begin to use representation as a means of communication.

❑ Respond to comments and questions, entering into dialogue about their creations.

### What you will need

Playdough; a table with a wipeable surface; a range of tools such as rolling pins, plastic shape cutters, plastic knives, an old garlic press.

### Getting ready

Make your own playdough, preferably involving the children. The following is an easy basic recipe:

❑ 2 cups of flour

❑ 1 cup of salt

❑ water, approximately 1 cup, but add little by little to get the consistency you want

❑ 2 tablespoons of cooking oil (gives a smooth texture, but leave out if you dislike the oiliness)

Knead all the ingredients together until you have the consistency of bread dough.

Divide the dough into separate balls and add different food colourings. The dough will keep indefinitely in an airtight tin.

### What to do

Show the children the playdough table and leave them to explore freely. Observe discreetly and choose when to introduce one or two tools and techniques, such as using a rolling pin and cutting the playdough with a plastic knife or a shape cutter. Your timing will depend on how well the child's fine motor movements are developing and the point at which interest is starting to wane.

Continue to introduce new tools and techniques to maintain interest in the playdough. See 'Clay techniques' below for some ideas. You may wish to look into some of the specialised playdough tools available, such as patterned rollers, wheel cutters or dough machines. If your budget is tight, you can substitute an old garlic press, a pastry wheel and rolling pins with grooves carved into the wood. You can also gather items such as Lego, Stickle bricks and cotton reels for pressing patterns into the dough - an activity that links conceptually with printing.

Setting up a semi-permanent table for playdough is ideal because the children can then choose to play with it whenever they wish. If you find the children start to lose interest, limit the times when it is available. If you find that the table is often overcrowded, add more tables. You can also hold planned playdough sessions with your group.

## Exploring clay

There is no substitute for the malleable texture of good, old-fashioned clay. Clay can be introduced in exactly the same way as playdough - introducing the practicalities, showing the children a few techniques and then leaving them to explore freely. The activity links with the same Stepping Stones as 'Exploring playdough'.

### What you will need

Balls of clay, stored in a plastic bag and an airtight tin; a table with a wipeable surface; a range of tools such as rolling pins, plastic shape cutters, plastic knives; overalls.

### Getting ready

Clay needs a bit of attention to keep it in a usable condition. It has a tougher consistency than playdough, so you do need to get it just right to ensure that the children can manipulate it easily. Store it well-wrapped in plastic in an airtight tin and start preparing it a day or two before you want to use it. If it has become a little hard, wrap small chunks in a damp towel. The absorbent clay soaks up the moisture and becomes workable - although clay that has completely dried out is difficult to rescue without specialised equipment.

Newclay is suitable for use with young children and should be available from your usual art supplier. It is reinforced with nylon fibres which makes it tough when dry, even without firing.

Roll the clay into balls for the children to use - between the size of a golf ball and a tennis ball is about right for most activities and projects.

### What to do

Introduce the clay and the clay table in the same way as the playdough and let the children explore freely.

If possible, leave the clay table, clay and tools out on semi-permanent display so that the children can choose to play with the clay whenever they wish. If you do this, you will need to remind the children to put on their overalls and wash their hands afterwards. You also need to show them how to take the clay out of the tin and return it after use (the clay will dry up if it is left out on the table for too long). Keep an eye on the tin to make sure the lid has been properly replaced.

If your group does not cope well with the practicalities of playing with clay independently, you can hold a planned group session instead.

## Clay techniques

Once your children have had lots of experience playing with and exploring clay, you can start to introduce some different techniques. The following activities are set out in approximate order of difficulty:

### Rolling a sausage

Give each child a small ball of soft clay. Show them how to roll the ball back and forth with the palms of the hand to make a sausage shape. This is the starting point for rolling a long, thin snake. With older ones, carry on rolling to make the sausage into a snake. Most children will need a bit of help with their snake.

### Rolling a pancake

Give each child a ball of soft clay. Show them how to flatten the ball slightly with the palm of their hand and then roll it out to make a pancake. Be ready to help if a child cannot press firmly or evenly enough with the rolling pin. If you have problems with the clay sticking to the board or table, roll onto a damp cloth (old muslin nappies are good). The cloth can then be peeled easily off the clay.

### Making a tile

Help the children to roll out balls of clay and cut them into tile shapes. Make sure that the clay is no thinner than 1 cm. Give the children various tools for making marks and patterns in the clay - glue spatulas, drinking straws, Lego or Stickle bricks, match sticks. Encourage older ones to create patterns by repeating marks. Point out that the children need to control their mark making movements so that the tool they are using does not slice right through the clay.

### Rolling a ball

Give each child a chunk of clay and show her how to roll the clay into a ball. The easiest technique is to roll the ball round and round between the two hands, cupping the ball in the lower hand to keep the spherical shape.

### Making a thumb pot

This activity is for older children with large hands and strong fingers. Show the child how to push the thumbs into the centre of a ball of clay and squeeze the sides to create a small pot. Be ready to help if necessary. Provide sponges dampened with water and show the children how to moisten a finger and use it to smooth the surface of the clay pot. The pot can then be decorated with marks and patterns or painted (see 'Painting and varnishing clay models' below). Use this technique for making divas for Diwali or little trinket pots for Christmas or Mother's Day presents.

### Making a coil pot

This activity is for older children with good hand-eye co-ordination. Roll out and cut some flat discs of clay and prepare lots of snakes. Show the children how to attach a snake to the disc by moistening the edge of the disc and pressing on the end of the snake until the clay bonds. The snake can then be coiled around to build up the sides of the pot. You can also show the children how to smooth the inside with a teaspoon handle, binding the coils together to strengthen the sides of the pot.

## Painting and varnishing clay models

Once a clay model has dried, it can be painted with thick, ready-mixed paint. When the paint has dried, the child can varnish her model with a solution of PVA glue mixed with water (approximately one part glue to four or five parts water.) Don't worry about the glue looking opaque. It becomes clear as it dries and adds a gentle glowing quality to the colours of the paint.

## Clay or playdough?

From a craft point of view, clay is the most versatile and satisfying modelling material to use. However, if some of your children find it too tough to work easily, you can introduce all the above techniques with playdough. The children can then progress onto clay as their hands develop the necessary size and strength.

## Constructing models from junk

Junk modelling offers a different experience from clay modelling because it involves joining separate parts rather than moulding a malleable material. At the pre-school stage, junk modelling also introduces a wider

range of technological challenges than clay. For example, how to balance the structure, how to support the different parts, ways of joining a variety of objects and discovering the properties of different shapes.

Junk modelling is a good way of recycling scrap items that would otherwise be thrown away. Talk to older children about this aspect of the activity and encourage them to bring in things from home to add to the junk box.

The activity links with the same Stepping Stones as 'Exploring playdough' and 'Exploring clay'.

### What you will need

A range of suitable junk, such as boxes, kitchen roll tubes, empty spice containers, yoghurt pots, milk bottle tops, drinking straws, pieces of string, wool, fabric scraps, tin foil and any other materials that can be safely be used for making models; glue; sticky tape; Blu-tak; scissors; thick paint; a large box for storage.

### Getting ready

Plan the joining techniques you want to show the children and make sure you have enough of each type of junk for all the children in the group to have a turn.

### What to do

Get the children started by introducing a couple of building techniques. For example, you could show them how to glue a kitchen roll on its side on top of a box, or tape a roll upright onto a box.

Once you have introduced the materials, let the children get on with exploring by themselves. Observe discreetly and step in with some help if a child is struggling. Your involvement does need to be monitored carefully, however. While you do not want to take away the opportunity for the child to solve problems for herself, you also do not want her to become frustrated to the point of giving up.

As much as possible, let the children come up with their own ideas. Talk to each child about what she wants to make and encourage her to plan her model. What pieces of junk is she going to use? How is she going to join the different parts? How can she decorate her model once it is finished?

If the children need some direction, suggest that they make a building or a vehicle. You can also challenge them to make the tallest tower they can manage, or use as many different shapes in their model as possible. A third possibility is to make a mobile. Keep the models small and provide lots of coloured paper and other materials for decoration. They can then be suspended from string and tied onto a wire coat-hanger or two pieces of wooden dowelling, joined to make a cross. Involve the children in assembling the mobiles so that they can make discoveries about balance.

If you have room in your setting, try to make the junk materials available for free choice on a regular basis as well as holding planned group activities.

### Assessment

❑ Observe the children to see how successfully they can co-ordinate hand movements to:

- roll out playdough/clay with a rolling pin
- roll a sausage
- roll a ball

All these activities demand an appropriate amount of hand pressure. Watch out for this and also observe how well a child adjusts to the different malleability of playdough and clay.

❑ Do the children understand how to use a shape cutter and can they co-ordinate and control their hand movements to:

- press down within the pancake?
- press down hard enough to cut right through the material?

❑ Junk modelling depends on being able to envisage a construction from the different scrap items available, select appropriate items and support, balance and join the separate pieces. Watch out for how successfully the children can combine and carry out these three activities.

❑ Look out for the degree of creativity and imagination the child brings to her modelling.

**Creative Development**

# Beat out that rhythm!

The child has been surrounded by rhythm from babyhood. Words, songs, music and nursery rhymes each have their own sound pattern. These activities highlight sound patterns and show the children how to beat out rhythms using clapping, body percussion and instruments. The body percussion activities (see below) can also be linked with the theme of 'All about me'.

Any singing and music activities provide a good opportunity to spot possible hearing loss, temporary or otherwise. If you are concerned about a particular child, suggest that parents request a hearing test.

## Clapping names

Clapping a child's name makes the simplest introduction to beating out a rhythm. Names are familiar words for the young child and they give everyone in the group a personal involvement in the activity.

The activity links with the following Stepping Stones:

❑ Respond to sound with body movement.

❑ Tap out simple repeated rhythms.

### Getting ready

Make a list of the children's names, dividing them into three sections - names with one beat (Kim, Joe, Josh), names with two beats (An-war, Ka-tie, Conn-or) and names with three beats (Chris-to-pher, Jess-i-ca, Sun-i-ta).

### What to do

Start off by clapping names with just one beat. Repeat the name and clap at the same time, encouraging the children to join in:

Kim/Kim/Kim/Kim - clap/clap/clap/clap

Work through the children's names, one by one, before moving onto names with two beats. Repeat the name a few times:

An-war/An-war/An-war - clap clap/clap clap/clap clap

Continue in the same way with three beats, making sure that every child's name has been clapped before you finish the activity.

When the children have mastered clapping single names, try putting two names together to make a more complex rhythm:

Kim/An-war - clap/clap clap

An-war/Chris-to-pher - clap clap/ clap clap clap

Ask the children to choose pairs of names and help them to clap the rhythm. Make sure you repeat each rhythm a few times to get across the idea of repeated sound patterns

**Early Learning Goals**

These activities will help you work towards the following goals:

❑ Recognise and explore how sounds can be changed, sing simple songs from memory, recognise repeated sounds and sound patterns.

❑ Express and communicate ideas, thoughts and feelings by using ... a variety of songs and musical instruments.

❑ Use imagination in ... music.

Kim Chris-to-pher/Kim Chris-to-pher/Kim Chris-to-pher

clap clap clap clap/clap clap clap clap/clap clap clap clap

You can work through these activities as slowly or quickly as you wish, depending on how easily the children pick up the idea of what to do.

If younger ones need to spend more time clapping single names, you could move on to surnames, the names of friends or relations, animals or any other source of words that might appeal to your group.

Stretch older ones by asking them if they can clap certain names without your help. Encourage them to come up with more complex combinations of names to clap.

## Clapping nursery rhymes

Like names, nursery rhymes combine familiarity with strong and satisfying rhythms. Once children are starting to master clapping the rhythms of their names, try clapping out the rhythms of some well-known nursery rhymes.

The activity links with the following Stepping Stones:

❑ Join in favourite songs/Sing a few simple, familiar songs/Begin to build a repertoire of songs.

❑ Respond to sound with body movement.

❑ Tap out simple repeated rhythms.

### Getting ready

Make a list of the nursery rhymes your children know well and put them into pairs of rhymes with distinctive and contrasting rhythms. For example, 'Humpty Dumpty' and 'Twinkle, Twinkle, Little Star'.

### What to do

Sing a familiar nursery rhyme, asking the children to join in. Sing the rhyme again and clap the rhythm, encouraging the children to join in with the clapping. Sing and clap a second nursery rhyme with a contrasting rhythm.

Help younger ones to develop the ability to clap out the rhythm by repeating the activity with a range of different rhymes and songs.

Challenge older ones to guess which of two contrasting rhymes you are clapping. Any children who are ready can clap one of two rhymes for the group to guess.

## Making rhythms with body percussion

Other parts of the body can be used to beat out the rhythm of a name or a nursery rhyme, following the same format as with clapping. There are endless ways in which the body can be used to create sounds. Try some of the following:

❑ stamping with foot

❑ hitting fist against palm

❑ tapping fingers against head

❑ slapping thighs

❑ slapping upper arms

❑ tapping foot against floor

Bear in mind that it is more challenging for the child to beat out a rhythm using body percussion than straightforward clapping.

The activity links with the same Stepping Stones as 'Clapping names' and 'Clapping nursery rhymes'.

### What to do

Let the children practise and enjoy making body sounds. When you feel they are ready, try beating out the rhythms of one, two and three syllable names with the body percussion sound.

When the children have mastered this activity, choose two names and ask the children to clap the rhythm of the names. Choose two different body percussions, for example, tapping head and stamping feet. Beat out the rhythm of the names with body percussion:

❑ Kim An-war - tap stamp stamp

Repeat a few times and then choose two different names and, if you wish, two different body percussion movements:

❑ Conn-or Jo-seph - slap slap clap clap

You can keep the activity simple by sticking to names with just one or two beats, as above. Alternatively, if some of your older children are picking up rhythms and remembering routines easily, you can introduce names with three beats:

❑ Ar-an Jenn-i-fer - stamp stamp tap tap tap

❑ Mad-e-line Sun-i-ta - slap slap slap punch punch punch

Practise the routine a number of times

ACTIVITY

so that the children will remember it and become more fluent. Don't give up if it does not work the first time. Most children will get the hang of it in the end - particularly if you are ready to laugh and enjoy all the times when you go wrong.

## The beginnings of musical notation

At this point, some older children may be ready to start representing the sound patterns you have created - a first experience of writing music.

This activity links with the following Stepping Stones:

❑ Tap out simple repeated rhythms and make some up.

❑ ... create movement in response to music/Begin to move rhythmically.

### What you will need

Cards with drawings of the different body percussion movements you have introduced to the children. For example, clapping hands, fingers tapping head, a stamping foot (see illustrations).

### What to do

Introduce the cards showing different movements. Make sure you have several copies of each one. Go through a name and body percussion routine and then ask a child 'How many stamps did we do?' Help her to count the stamps and choose a corresponding number of cards. Set them out in a line, then count the next number of movements: 'How many punches did we do?' Set them out next to the 'stamp' cards. Look at the line with the children and 'read' it, reproducing the routine once again.

If possible, leave your musical notation undisturbed and use it to remind you and the children of the rhythm you created the day before. This makes the point that musical notation is a record and enables us to remember and repeat the music we composed on a previous occasion.

Some older children may be ready to compose their own rhythms. Show them how to choose a series of pictures and set them out in a line. Ensure that the rhythm does not

become too complicated. Limit them to two different movements, encouraging them to choose two or three of the same movement to get across the idea of a sound pattern and repeated sound (stamp stamp punch or slap slap slap tap tap). Try out the rhythms the children have composed, making sure you repeat them a few times to emphasise that this is a sound pattern.

## Other activities

All of these activities can also be done using percussion instruments. Give the children different instruments. They can then beat out a name on their instruments one at a time or play the names all together. Alternatively, you can create a more complex activity by asking children with different instruments to beat out separate parts of the rhythm. For example:

- ❑ An-war Kim - triangle triangle cymbal
- ❑ Chris-to-pher Jo-seph - drum drum drum bells bells

Try beating out the rhythm quickly and slowly. Start off with simple clapping names and introduce different speeds to other rhythm activities if the children are ready.

Play clapping games such as 'pat-a-cake'. Younger ones can simply hold up their hands while an adult does the clapping, gradually participating as they become able to pick up the pattern of movement and co-ordinate their own hand movements.

### Assessment

- ❑ Children vary enormously in their ability to recognise and beat out a rhythm. Look out for how easily the child can pick up the beats in a name and co-ordinate clapping her hands. Most children should be able to listen to, assimilate and clap the rhythm of a simple nursery rhyme by the time they leave your setting.
- ❑ Assess whether older ones can recognise the beats in a name by clapping a name with one, two or three beats and asking them: 'Whose name am I clapping?'
- ❑ Look out for how well the children can make body percussion sounds, use them to follow a rhythm and switch from one movement to the next - slap slap/punch.

# High, low, soft and loud

These activities introduce pitch and volume to the children. Pitch is the highness or lowness of a note and volume is the quietness or loudness of the music being played. As well as introducing musical elements, the activities encourage the children to develop their listening skills.

The activities begin at a simple level, using both the singing voice and the speaking voice to express high/low and loud/quiet. You can then progress to playing high notes and low notes on the chime bars or piano and show the children how to use percussion and other instruments to make a loud or a soft sound. If you have older children who are starting to create their own sound pictures, they can be encouraged to introduce these elements to their music.

Through playing names with chime bars, the children are introduced to the beginnings of playing simple tunes. Through exploring loud and soft sounds with musical instruments, the children are introduced to the idea of music as a means of expressing the imagination and representing different thoughts and ideas.

## High voices, low voices

This is a simple introduction to high sounds and low sounds using the singing voice. To help the children grasp the concept, the activity links upwards movements with ascending notes and downwards movements with descending notes.

The activity contributes to the following Stepping Stones:

❑ Respond to sound with body movement/Imitate and create movement in response to music.

❑ Explore and learn how sounds can be changed.

### Getting ready

Prepare a list of commands, linked with an upward movement or a downward movement. Put the commands into pairs, such as:

❑ please stand up/crouch down low

❑ stretch up to the sky/curl up on the floor

❑ tap your head/tickle your toes

❑ reach up high/bow down low

### What to do

Start off by singing pairs of commands to the children. Use ascending notes to sing the upwards commands and descending notes for the downwards commands. Remind the children to listen carefully to the commands. If necessary, ask a helper to join in to prompt the little ones.

Move on to singing the full scale of C major, progressing through the notes from low to high. Give the children a 'growing' scenario such as tiny seeds growing into a plant and ask them to curl up on the floor. Sing doh, ray, me, fah, so, lah, tee, doh. As the notes you sing get higher and higher the children uncurl and stretch upwards.

Try the activity a few times, introducing different movements such as a cat waking up and stretching itself or pretending to climb up a ladder, or a butterfly emerging from its chrysalis. Can the children think of any upwards movements?

## High and low notes on the piano

This activity progresses from using a high/low voice to playing high and low notes on the piano or chime bars. It links with the following Stepping Stone:

❑ Explore the different sounds of instruments.

**Early Learning Goals**

These activities will help you work towards the following goals:

❑ Recognise and explore how sounds can be changed, sing simple songs from memory, recognise repeated sounds and sound patterns.

❑ Express and communicate ideas, thoughts and feelings by using ... a variety of songs and musical instruments.

❑ Respond in a variety of ways to what they ... hear.

❑ Use imagination in ... music.

### What you will need

A piano or chime bars (C, D, E, F, G, A, B, C).

### What to do

Show the children the high notes and the low notes on the piano or the chime bars. Ask them to listen carefully to the difference and use the terms 'high note' and 'low note' as much as possible.

Progress from clapping the beats in the children's names (see 'Beat out that rhythm: Clapping names', page 34) to playing the children's names. Start out with just two chime bars or piano notes - E and G. Choose a name with one beat and play it with a single note:

Jo/Jo/Jo/Jo

E/E/E/E

Continue until you have played all the single beat names and then progress to names with two beats, using two notes to play the name:

Ped-ro / Ped-ro / Ped-ro / Ped-ro

E G / E G / E G / E G

Move on to names with three beats - Chris-to-pher
G G E

Show the children how to play their own names. If you are using chime bars, give the children two beaters and encourage them to use alternate hands. Ask the rest of the group to sing or clap along with the child who is playing her name. If clapping drowns out the chime bars, choose a quieter body percussion movement.

Develop the activity as slowly or as quickly as you wish.

Give younger children plenty of freedom to explore and play with the piano and chime bars.

Challenge older children to create more complex combinations of names: Chris-to- pher Jo-seph / Chris-to-pher Jo-seph. Introduce other chime bar notes for them to play.

## The beginnings of musical notation

This is an activity for older children who are demonstrating the ability to distinguish between high notes and low notes and are able to play names and combinations of names on the chime bars or piano (see 'High and low notes on the piano').

### What you will need

Card strips with coloured stickers showing simple tunes for older ones to play; small cards showing a single colour sticker; piano or chime bars with coloured stickers stuck to the keys.

### Getting ready

Prepare card strips with coloured stickers showing simple tunes. For example, 'Baa, Baa, Black Sheep' could be:

yellow yellow red red green orange blue green red

brown brown purple purple pink pink yellow

Stick corresponding coloured stickers onto the keys of the piano or chime bars and prepare lots of single cards with matching colours.

### What to do

Introduce the children to the cards with coloured spots showing simple tunes. Show them how to match the colours with the piano keys or chime bars and play the notes accordingly. Can they recognise the tune? Give them plenty of opportunity to practise.

If the children cope well with this

activity, show them how to put the single cards in a sequence of notes and then play their sound picture on the piano or chime bars. Encourage them to keep the sequence simple and include some repeated notes.

Stick or Blu-tak the sequence of cards to a strip of paper so they can be kept. This shows the children that musical notation enables them (or anyone else) to play the same sound picture whenever they wish. You can also record them playing their sound pictures on cassette tape. Encourage them to think of a name for their composition.

## Loud voices, soft voices

This simple activity introduces loud sounds and soft sounds. It is useful for starting off a music session or slipping into the few minutes before snack time. It is suitable for all ages with younger ones following the lead of the older ones.

The activity links with the following Stepping Stone:

- ❑ Explore and learn how sounds can be changed.

### Getting ready

Prepare a series of questions that involve answering in different volumes:

- ❑ Have you brought your speaking voice? Yes, we have. (in normal speaking voice)
- ❑ Have you brought your singing voice? Yes, we have. (sung)
- ❑ Have you brought your whispering voice? Yes, we have. (whispered)
- ❑ Have you brought your shouting voice? Yes, we have. (shouted)
- ❑ Have you brought your quiet voice? Yes, we have. (said quietly but not in a whisper)
- ❑ Have you brought your loud voice? Yes, we have. (said loudly but not in a shout)

### What to do

Simply ask one of the questions using an appropriate voice and encourage the children to respond in a similar voice. If you have a lively group, you may prefer to leave out the shouting question.

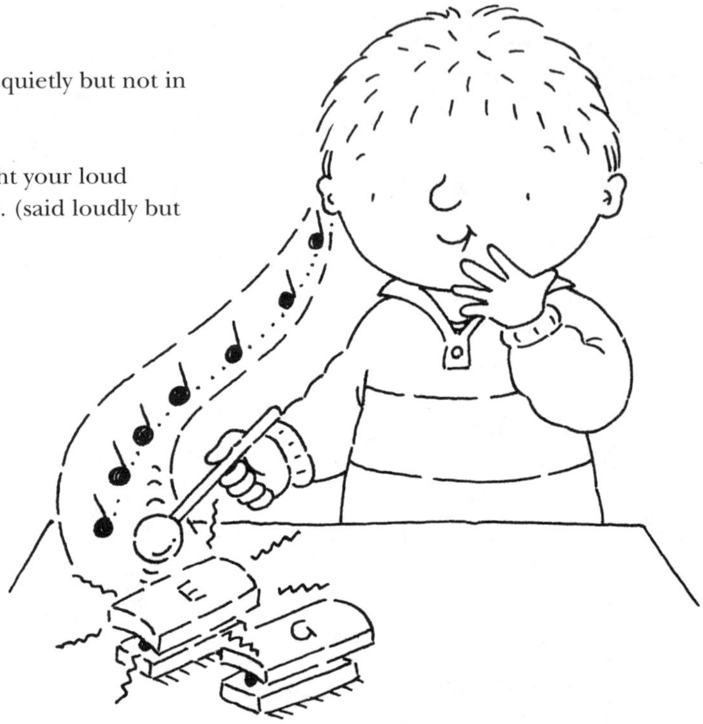


## Loud singing, soft singing

This activity progresses from loud/quiet voices to loud/quiet singing, introducing the concept of a conductor whose movements tell the singer how to perform.

The activity links with the following Stepping Stones:

- ❑ Join in favourite songs/Sing a few simple, familiar songs/Begin to build a repertoire of songs.

### Getting ready

Make a list of songs the children know inside out and a list of songs that suit being sung loudly or softly, such as 'The Grand Old Duke of York' (loudly) or 'Hush-a-bye Baby' (softly).

### What to do

Sing a song the children know really well, asking them to join in. Position yourself in front of the group and ask everyone to stand up. As you lift your arms, the song should be sung louder and louder. As you lower your arms, the song should be sung softer and softer. The children have to watch carefully and control their voices. Ask a helper to lead the children while they are getting the idea of what to do.

You can make this activity as simple or complex as you wish:

- ❑ With younger ones, concentrate simply on the singing. As they become able to modulate their voices, you can introduce singing one part of the song loudly and one part softly. Encourage them to listen to you as you sing loudly and softly.
- ❑ Older ones can be challenged to get louder and louder or softer and softer as you gradually raise or lower your arms. As the children become increasingly able to modulate their voices, you can introduce lots of changes within the one song. You can also ask an older child to do the conducting.

## Loud music, soft music

Having explored loud/soft voices and loud/soft singing, the children can progress to playing instruments loudly or softly. In order to get the most from this activity, the children should be familiar with the instruments and how they are played.

This activity links with the following Stepping Stones:

❑ Show an interest in the way musical instruments sound/Explore the different sounds of instruments.

❑ Explore and learn how sounds can be changed.

❑ Try to capture experiences and responses with music ...

### What you need

A variety of percussion instruments - drums, tambourines, cymbals, triangles, castanets, rhythm sticks, bells, chime bars, shakers; the piano.

### What to do

Explore the percussion instruments and look at how we make a loud sound and how we make a soft sound - beating the drum hard, beating the drum softly; shaking the shakers firmly, shaking the shakers gently.

Sing 'I am the Music Man' with the children, working through each instrument. Add a second verse about playing the instrument loudly or softly:

I can play it louder, LOUDER, **LOUDER**

I can play it very loud, VERY LOUD like this.

Ask the children to play their instruments loudly for this verse. Older ones may be able to increase their volume with each 'louder'. Do exactly the same with 'softer'.

You can also introduce different scenarios to represent loud and soft:

❑ A herd of elephants, scampering mice.

❑ A lumbering giant, a tiptoeing fairy.

❑ Feeling angry; feeling peaceful and quiet.

Talk about each scenario with the children. What do you do and say when you feel angry or peaceful and quiet? How would a giant sound as he lumbered through the forest? Older ones may be able to think of some words to describe the sound made by a herd of elephants. Choose different instruments to express the different sounds - the cymbals and drums for feeling angry, the shakers and triangle for feeling peaceful. Practise making loud sounds and soft sounds and then go on to suggest each scenario. Can the children make their instruments sound like a herd of elephants charging through the jungle? (play as loudly as possible). Can they sound like a tiny mouse scuttling through the house? (play as quietly as possible.)

With your younger children, concentrate on learning how to play the instruments and developing the ability to follow instructions such as 'start playing' and 'stop playing.' Gradually introduce the idea of beating, shaking or rattling hard or gently to create loud and soft sounds.

Older ones can be challenged to vary their loudness or softness. You can use the raising and lowering arms technique as with 'Loud singing, soft singing'. You can also give them a scenario that needs them to get louder and louder then softer and softer - the herd of elephants getting nearer and nearer and then further and further away.

Throughout the activities, use appropriate words to describe playing the instruments: beat the drum; rattle the shakers; clash the cymbals; shake the tambourine; strike the triangle ...

## Other activities

❑ Show the children the loud and soft pedals on the piano and leave them to explore.

❑ Show the children the volume button on the radio or cassette recorder.

❑ Fill empty spice pots with different substances that make a loud or soft sound, relative to each other when shaken. For example, marbles or small pebbles make a loud sound, sand makes a soft sound, dried peas or beans make a medium sound. Make pairs of cylinders and ask the children to match them by sound alone.

❑ If you have children who are starting to compose their own little tunes (see 'The beginnings of musical notation') encourage them to think about whether they want to play notes loudly or softly. Show them how to strike the chime bar firmly or gently.

### Assessment

❑ Look out for how well the child can modulate her voice to make a loud/soft or high/low sound. By the time they leave your setting, most children should be able to distinguish and reproduce loud/soft sounds and high/low notes through singing and playing musical instruments.

❑ Look out for how well the child responds to representing different scenarios with loud sounds or soft sounds. Has the child grasped the idea of communicating an idea through sound? Can she suggest scenarios of her own to play?

Creative Development

# Exploring musical instruments

These activities introduce the children to a wide range of musical instruments, encouraging them to explore and discover the different ways in which each instrument is played. Musical instruments can offer unique possibilities to children with special needs. Children with hearing impairment can gain a positive experience through feeling the vibrations of the different instruments while children with sight impairment can be given particular encouragement to feel as well as listen. The activities culminate in the creation of a music display. Encourage the children to use their ever increasing skills and imagination to plan and produce pictures, models and objects to add to the display. Whereas younger ones can enjoy looking at and exploring the things on display, older ones can play a pivotal role in the planning and setting up.

**Early Learning Goals**

These activities will help you work towards the following goals:

❑ Recognise and explore how sounds can be changed.

❑ Express and communicate ideas, thoughts and feelings by using ... a variety of musical instruments.

❑ Use imagination in ... music.

❑ Respond in a variety of ways to what they see, hear, smell, touch and feel.

## Looking at instruments

This activity encourages the child to explore and become familiar with different musical instruments, using all the senses. It links with the following Stepping Stones:

❑ Show an interest in the way musical instruments sound.

❑ Explore and learn how sounds can be changed.

❑ Explore the different sounds of instruments.

### What you will need

Gather as many instruments as possible. If you have difficulty collecting a variety, you can build up groups of instruments by adding pictures. Aim for at least one instrument from each of the main groups:

❑ woodwind - oboe, clarinet, recorder

❑ brass - tuba, horn, trumpet

❑ string - violin, cello, guitar

❑ keyboard - piano

❑ percussion - drums, castanets, triangles, cymbals

Try to include instruments from different cultures: maracas and panpipes from South America, castanets from Spain, rattle drums from China, sitars from India, conical drums from Africa. These can either be displayed as a group of instruments from other countries or added to the relevant category - sitar with the strings, panpipes with the wind instruments, and so on.

### What to do

Choose two or three instruments at a time, depending on how many you have managed to collect. Keep your group as small as possible so that each child has plenty of opportunity to explore the instruments. Talk first of all about how delicate and precious the instrument is and how we must be very careful with it. Supervise the children closely but at the same time encourage them to touch and smell as well as look. Musical instruments are designed to be handled and many instruments, such as violins, have a distinctive smell.

Show the children how to get a sound from the instrument. Show them how the sound is changed: pressing a finger on the violin string before drawing the bow across the strings, or on a guitar string before plucking; pressing a finger on the keys of a clarinet or the holes of a recorder before blowing.

Explore all the different parts of the instrument and accessories such as the rosin for treating violin bows, reeds for use with clarinets and soft cloths for dusting and polishing the instruments.

Let younger ones simply explore and enjoy looking, touching and listening, always supervising carefully. Refer to the instrument by name as much as possible.

Name the different parts of the instrument with older ones - bridge, bow, string, chin rest, rosin (violin); mouthpiece, valves, bell (horn). See how many names they can remember from one day to the next.

## Listening to live music

There is no substitute for the experience of listening to music played live. Invite musicians to bring in their instruments and play for the children. Ask parents, friends and any local amateur orchestras or music groups for contacts. Get in touch with your local primary or secondary school and ask if there are any young musicians willing to play for your group.

Try to cover a range of different instruments. If visiting musicians have not had experience of playing and talking to the pre-school age group, give some pointers. Are they happy to allow the children to touch and play their instrument? What interesting sound effects can they create with their instruments? Ask them to play some well-known tunes that the children can sing, dance or clap to.

## Listening to recorded music

Learning how to sit quietly and listen to recorded music is an important part of the child's musical development. This activity also helps the children discover the nature and purpose of recorded music: how the tape recorder or CD player is operated and the fact that this technology enables you to listen to the same piece of music again and again - in contrast with the visiting musician.

### What you will need

Music cassette tapes or CDs; a cassette recorder or CD player; if possible, the instrument corresponding with the recorded music you are planning to play; comfortable cushions or mats.

### Getting ready

Gather a collection of tapes or CDs featuring the instruments you have been looking at. Try to include a range of musical styles - classical, jazz, folk, rock and music from different cultures. Look in the music section of your local library. If you want to introduce music from different countries, the *Rough Guide* produces a series of CDs featuring traditional music and dance from a wide range of countries, continents, cultures and genres.

Choose a time of day when the children are alert but calm. Check that you have the tape wound to the point at which you want to start playing, or that you know in advance the number of the CD track.

### What to do

Settle the children on the cushions or mats. Remind them of any related experience, such as a visit from a musician. If possible, show them the instrument or instruments they are about to listen to.

Explain to the children that you are all going to listen to some music. Encourage them to sit as quietly and as still as possible and to shut their eyes.

Play the music for a couple of minutes. Stop playing as soon as the group gets restless. If you want to continue the session, let the children have a wriggle before they settle down to listen again.

Concentrate on encouraging the younger ones to sit quietly with eyes closed and listen to the music. Point out the cassette recorder or CD player and help them discover that the music is coming from the machine. Ask one of the little ones to help you in pressing the start button and the stop button.

Talk about the music with the older ones. Did they like it? How did it make them feel? What did they think about when they were listening? Prompt them with your own thoughts and responses if necessary.

## A musical instrument display

An interactive music display provides a focal point for all the music activities in

your setting. Apart from giving older children the chance to join in with planning and setting up a display, it is a good means of enabling the children to explore a range of different activities through free choice play. If your display is comprehensive, it will link with just about all the music-related Stepping Stones.

### What you will need

As many instruments as possible, including home-made (see 'Making musical instruments' pages 46-49); posters, pictures and postcards of instruments and musicians; paper, pencils, crayons and paints; music notation paper; tapes of music and a cassette player; headphones; a comfortable floor cushion; a large table for the display; boxes in various sizes draped with cloths for displaying instruments.

### Getting ready

Prepare an overall plan for your display and the different sections. For example, instruments (both interactive and for looking at only), pictures, models, tape recorder and tapes. Think through the best place to set up the display. If possible, choose a location away from the main part of the room where listening to tapes and playing instruments will not disturb the rest of the group - otherwise you may need to limit free access to the percussion instruments. It can also be useful to position the table next to a high shelf for displaying delicate instruments safely out of reach, or near the piano. If your setting is non-permanent, plan the display so that it can be easily set up and dismantled.

Check that your table is large enough for all you want to show and that there is space for displaying pictures - either on an adjacent wall or board. Check also that you have room near the table for floor cushions and tape recorder and that your display boxes are sturdy enough to hold the instruments.

### What to do

Explain to the children that you are going to make a music display with instruments, pictures, posters, music to listen to, drawings and models. Explain that some parts of the display can only be looked at (such as the delicate violin), while other parts can be played with (such as the percussion instruments).

Explain to the older ones that there will be written notices telling people about all the different things in the display and that you will need their help in planning what to write. Also explain that there will be a board for putting up pictures, posters, drawings and paintings.

Encourage older ones to make their own suggestions and bring in things from home. If necessary, send home a note explaining the display and giving some ideas for contributions.

### Displaying instruments

Start off by showing the children the instruments that will be displayed. Depending on age and previous experience, you could discuss with the children how to group the instruments. For example, if you have a good collection, you could make a string group, a wind group and a percussion group. Alternatively, you could organise the instruments into those that can be plucked, those that can be beaten and those that can be blown.

Sort out the delicate instruments that are for display only and those that can be played whenever the children wish. Include home-made instruments (see 'Making musical instruments' pages 46-49).

Display the instruments that are not to be touched on boxes of different sizes, draped with cloths. Place the delicate instruments at the back of the table or on a shelf. Place the instruments that can be played at the front of the table with a notice inviting children to explore them. Write out labels for the display, naming the instruments. Encourage the children to help you word little invitations and challenges such as:

❑ Come and play with these instruments.

❑ Please do not touch these instruments.

❑ Can you make a loud sound with the shaker?

❑ Can you beat the drum softly?

If you have any writers in your setting, ask them to help with writing labels and notices.

Change the interactive part of the display from time to time. Keep a few instruments back and swap them around to renew the children's interest. You can also change the written challenges:

❑ Choose an instrument and march like a soldier.

❑ Which instrument makes the loudest sound?

❑ Which instrument makes the softest sound?

Draw the children's attention to the changes and read through the new challenges with them. If necessary, keep reminding them of the challenges and take small groups to the table to try out the activities.

## Pictures, posters, drawings and paintings

Show the children the pictures you have collected and ask the children to help you sort them into groups for the display, such as large/small pictures, people playing instruments or different types of instruments. Plan and write out labels for the pictures. Involve the children in mounting the pictures - choosing the colour of sugar paper, sticking the picture onto the mount (unless the picture is precious) and decorating mounting papers (see 'Painting' on pages 62-65 and 'Printing' on pages 24-25 for some ideas.)

If you have a group of older children who are interested in observational drawing, put out paper, pencils and a still-life set piece made up of a couple of instruments. Encourage the children to sit down and draw the instruments, changing the still-life from time to time to rekindle interest.

## Listening to tapes

Introduce the tape recorder and headphones to the children. Show them how to use the headphones and how to play and stop the tape, the volume button, and the rewind. Show them the cushion to sit on and the tapes that they can listen to. Make just two or three tapes available, choosing a variety such as nursery rhymes, a violin concerto and traditional Indian music. Glue pictures onto the box to identify the music - a small picture of a violin or Humpty Dumpty. Make sure the children can identify which tape is which. Change the tapes from time to time to maintain interest. If you have older children, include some blank tapes so that they can record their own singing and playing with the instruments. Ensure that the children are clear about the difference between the blank tapes and the music tapes and keep a discreet eye on proceedings if the children are using the tapes independently.

## What else?

These are only suggestions. Your display should be flexible and should represent the interests of you and your group and the particular music activities you have been doing. It should also be the children's display. Other things you could add include: models of musical instruments made from clay, Plasticene, junk or any other modelling material; cards with note names or coloured stickers corresponding to stickers on piano keys or chime bars (see 'High, low, soft and loud: The beginnings of musical notation' on pages 39-40); musical scores and music notation paper for the children to explore; a music stand; a box of objects that make interesting noises such as a bunch of keys, a jar of peppercorns, two spoons.

### Assessment

❑ Look out for the extent to which the child uses all the senses in exploring the instruments. Observe younger ones to ensure that they can hold the instrument correctly in order to get sound from it. Are older ones able to create and change sound from a range of different instruments?

❑ Older children should be able to group some instruments according to how they are played (plucked, beaten, blown) or their traditional groupings (string, wind, percussion, keyboard).

❑ Make a note of how the children build up their repertoire of names for instruments. Can older children identify the different parts?

❑ Observe the children as they listen to music and make a note of how absorbed they appear to be. Bear in mind that fidgeting does not necessarily mean that a child is not listening or enjoying the experience. How do older children respond to talking about the music once it is finished?

❑ Observe the children as they interact with the music display. These moments of free time can sometimes tell you more about a child's capabilities and interests than participating in a planned activity.

Creative Development

# Making musical instruments

Making musical instruments helps the child progress towards many of the Early Learning Goals. Craft and design, using appropriate materials and tools, working with all the senses, exploring how sound is created, changed and made into music and creative expression are just some of the learning outcomes that emerge from this activity.

The activity can be as simple or as complex as you wish to make it. Even very young children can be helped to make some of the more simple instruments, and encouraged to explore and play with them.

## Making musical instruments

There are several approaches you can take to making musical instruments. If you choose to make just one or two instruments, you can choose examples to suit the age and development level of your children. You might want to concentrate on one group of instruments or choose one from each group. The easiest way to categorise home-made instruments is according to how they are played. The groups below cover plucking, shaking, beating, chiming and scraping.

Before making any of the following, look at some real instruments of a similar type. For example, show the children some maracas before making shakers; explore a guitar before making a plucking box; play the chime bars before making water chimes or cutlery chimes.

These activities link with the following Stepping Stones:

- ❑ Show an interest in the way musical instruments sound/Explore and learn how sounds can be changed/Explore the different sounds of instruments.
- ❑ Make three-dimensional structures.
- ❑ Work creatively on a small or large scale.
- ❑ Understand that different media can be combined.
- ❑ Show an interest in what they see, hear ... touch and feel/Further explore an experience using a range of senses.

**Early Learning Goals**

These activities will help you work towards the following goals:

- ❑ Explore ... shape, form and space in ... three dimensions.
- ❑ Recognise and explore how sounds can be changed.
- ❑ Express and communicate ideas, thoughts and feelings by using a widening range of materials, suitable tools ... (and) a variety of musical instruments.
- ❑ Use imagination in ... music.
- ❑ Respond in a variety of ways to what they see, hear, smell, touch and feel.

❑ Use one object to represent another, even when the objects have few characteristics in common.

❑ Respond to comments and questions, entering into dialogue about their creations.

## Plucking

### Plucking box

You will need boxes of different sizes, rubber bands of different lengths and thicknesses or pieces of elastic. The box must have one open side, such as a shoe box. Show the children how to stretch the rubber bands or tie lengths of elastic around the box. Experiment with different sounds by using rubber bands of different thicknesses. Compare finger plucking with using a plectrum or similar small flat object. If you put the bands close together, you can try strumming. Extend the art and craft element of the activity by decorating the box before attaching the strings. Try painting the box with thick paint or covering it with sheets of sugar paper. Have a look at the decorative patterns on a guitar and get older children to print patterns onto the box, or stick small pieces of paper around the edge.

Introduce words such as pluck, twang, strum, high, low, loud and soft.

## Shaking

### Shakers

You will need lidded tubs such as empty spice containers, yoghurt pots or film canisters and a range of different substances such as rice, beans, gravel, sand and marbles. Avoid red kidney beans, which are toxic if uncooked. Show the children how to fill the pots and make sure the lids are firmly screwed and taped down. Compare the sounds made by different substances. You can also introduce containers made from other materials. Try a wooden box, a small biscuit tin, a glass jar (for a light material such as sand: supervise closely.)

### Tambourines

You will need paper plates, milk bottle tops, a darning needle, strong thread and a hole puncher. Begin by decorating the paper plates with felt pens or collage. Check that collage pieces have been firmly stuck on so that they do not drop off when the tambourine is used. Show the children how to thread several milk bottle tops together to make bundles. Punch holes in the rim of the plate and tie the

bundles on to the rim. The tambourine can then be shaken or tapped. Encourage the children to dance with the tambourine and shake it high and low like a Latin dancer.

Introduce words such as loud, soft, quiet, noisy, rattle, shake.

## Beating

### Drums

You will need tubs or old saucepans with handles, sheets of greaseproof or parchment paper (the stronger, the better), strong, large rubber bands, wooden spoons, chopsticks and other beating instruments. Cut the greaseproof paper into circles large enough to stretch over the opening of the tub, with a good overlap. Secure the paper with the elastic band. Experiment with different beaters and encourage the children to find their own to try. You can also show the children different ways of holding the drum: attach a string to hang it round the neck like a military drum in a marching band; place it on the floor between the legs like an African drum; use a saucepan with a handle so that the drum can be held with one hand and beaten with the other like a tabor. If you want to decorate the drum, use felt pens to draw patterns on the greaseproof paper before attaching it to the tub.

### Rhythm sticks

You will need lengths of wooden dowelling, preferably in different diameters. Cut the dowelling into lengths, sanding the ends to make sure they do not give the children splinters. Show the children how to beat out rhythms by knocking the sticks together. Decorate the sticks with paint and varnish, leaving the ends plain. You can also make handles by showing the children how to glue lengths of felt or leather around the opposite ends.

Introduce words such as beat, drumstick, skin (the part of the drum that is beaten), loud, soft.

ACTIVITY

## Chiming

### Cutlery chimes

You will need a ball of string, spoons, knives and forks of different sizes (check that the knives and forks are not too sharp), a small table and Blu-tak or Plasticene. Tie lengths of string around the cutlery handles and attach the strings to a longer piece. Turn a small table upside down and suspend the cutlery between two of the legs, keeping the string as taut as possible. If all the spoons slide towards the middle, wedge lumps of Plasticene or Blu-tak on either side of each knot. Involve the children as much as possible in making the chimes. When the chimes are finished, show them how to strike the spoons with a spare spoon or fork. Experiment with the sounds made by different sizes and types of cutlery.

### Water chimes

You will need empty milk bottles, a funnel and a jug of water. Show older children how to fill the milk bottles using a funnel, emphasising that you only pour a small amount at a time. Make sure that each bottle has a different amount from the rest, including one that is full and one that is empty. Show the children how to make notes by striking the bottle with a striking implement. Experiment with different strikers such as a wooden spoon, a metal spoon, a pencil or a large plastic knitting needle. You can also encourage older children to find their own strikers to try.

Highlight that the volume of water changes the note by filling and then emptying a bottle little by little, striking it each time.

The activity as a whole can be linked to the theme of 'Water'.

Introduce words such as strike, chime, loud, soft, high note, low note, full, empty.

## Scraping

### Sandpaper scrapers

You will need chunks of wood, coarse sandpaper and PVA glue. Stick sandpaper onto the chunks of wood and show the children how to rub them together to make a scraping sound. If you wish, you can decorate the wood with paint and varnish.

## Playing the instruments

Use the song 'I am the Music Man' as a format for introducing and focussing on each instrument. In order to sing the song you need to give the instruments a name. Discuss this with older children - for example, water chimes could also be named milk bottle chimes, a plucking box could also be a shoe-box guitar. Alternatively, the names need not bear any relation to the instrument itself. Let the imagination run riot!

You can also use the home-made instruments for rhythm activities and loud and soft activities (see pages 37 and 40-41). The water chimes can be used to demonstrate high notes and low notes.

## Make a display

Add the home-made instruments to your music display (see pages 43-44). Alternatively, you can make a special display. Ask the children to lie down on a large sheet of paper in positions that tally with playing the particular instruments you have made. Cut out the body shapes and paint or sponge print, involving the children as much as possible (see 'Making a frieze', pages 68-69, for more ideas). Pin the pictures to the wall and attach the instruments. Make labels giving the special name you have created for each instrument: Akash is playing the shoe-box guitar; Melissa is playing the sandpaper scrapers. Where the instrument cannot be attached, such as the water chimes, ask older ones to draw and cut out pictures.

## Other activities

❑ Once you have introduced a few techniques for making instruments, put out various materials so that the children can make instruments by themselves. Include boxes, rubber bands, lidded tubs and substances to go inside, sticks, sandpaper pieces and so on. Try to add some other options. For example, a new substance to go inside a shaker or a different material to stretch over a tub to make a drum.

❑ Encourage the children to find everyday objects that make interesting and contrasting noises. See if you can find objects that use all the different movements - plucking, shaking, beating, chiming and scraping. For example, shaking car keys, plucking a hair band or hair elastic (with the permission of its owner), running a zip back and forth or rubbing two pine cones together to make a scraping sound. Try beating out rhythms with these different objects. Challenge your older ones to go on a sound safari in the setting or garden and see how many different sounds they can discover (see 'Taste, touch and smell journeys', pages 50-53).

**Assessment**

❑ These activities give you a good opportunity to observe how well the children can use art and craft skills such as cutting, sticking, painting and constructing. Once the children start to play their instruments you can also look out for whether they are able to handle them with care.

❑ Making instruments gives the older child an in-depth opportunity to discover how different sounds are created. Watch out for signs that the child understands how to pluck, beat, shake or scrape, depending on the nature of the instrument.

❑ Look out for how creatively a child decorates her instruments and how fully she explores the materials when given the chance to construct her own instrument.

# Taste, touch and smell journeys

The Early Learning Goals for Creative Development quite rightly highlight the role of the senses and the child's response to what they can see, hear, smell, touch and feel. Interestingly, they do not refer to taste. This is probably because we should not encourage young children to go around tasting their surroundings! You can, however, introduce some controlled tasting activities to develop the child's awareness of taste. At the same time, you can emphasise the importance of never putting anything strange in your mouth.

These activities start off with some games designed to focus on taste, smell and touch. You can then take the children on touching and smelling journeys around the room or garden. Older children can follow up their journeys by making touch and smell maps.

## Taste games

Use the following games with the children to highlight their sense of taste. All the games can be adapted for different ages and older ones can be encouraged to talk about their reactions to the taste experiences. With all tasting activities, check first for allergies. Make sure that any utensils are clean and provide separate implements for each child. Cocktail sticks are good, but they should only be used under close adult supervision.

The activities link with the following Stepping Stones:

❑ Show an interest in what they see, hear, smell, touch and feel/Further explore an experience using a range of senses.

❑ Use body language, gestures, facial expression or words to indicate personal satisfaction or frustration.

❑ Make comparisons.

### Food tasting tests

Choose some well-known foods with contrasting tastes and textures, such as bread, apple and chocolate. Ask the children to shut their eyes or use a blindfold and see if they can guess each food from taste alone. Some children are reluctant to taste something they can't see or a food that is unfamiliar. Don't push them to participate - encourage them to smell instead. You can also put aside pieces of food reserved for feeling rather than tasting. This, along with sniffing and looking, will utilise all five senses in exploring the foods.

Younger children can simply enjoy the experience of tasting, smelling and naming the foods. They can also be encouraged to think about whether they like or dislike a particular taste.

Older children can expand on taste likes and dislikes, as well as guessing the food. Encourage them to use different facial expressions and gestures in response to the tastes. Introduce taste and texture words such as sweet, salty, bitter, sour, crunchy, smooth, lumpy.

**Early Learning Goals**

These activities will help you work towards the following goals:

❑ Explore ... texture, shape, form and space in two and three dimensions.

❑ Respond in a variety of ways to what they ... smell, touch and feel.

❑ Express and communicate their ideas, thoughts and feelings by using a widening range of materials, suitable tools ... designing and making.

### Fruit tasting tests

Do the same as with 'Food tasting tests', using different fruits. This is a little more challenging because the flavours and textures of fruit do not offer such clear contrasts as bread, chocolate and apple. You can also try the activity with different drinks - milk, juice, squash, lemonade.

### The four basic tastes

The four basic tastes are sweet, salt, sour and bitter. Make up a salt solution, a sugar solution, lemon juice and grapefruit juice. Use a pipette to place a few drops on a child's tongue and, at the same time, name each taste. Let the children take sips of water from their own plastic cup, in between the different tastes. Encourage responses to the taste experiences, particularly facial expressions.

Older children can sort foods into

sweet and salty tastes. Choose foods such as tinned fruit, cheese, biscuits (sweet and savoury). You could also try a sour and bitter category although these tastes are harder for young children to distinguish than sweet and salt.

### Creating sandwiches

Talk about favourite foods and the kinds of foods children eat at home. What foods normally go together within a meal? What do the children eat in their sandwiches?

With older children you can make up some creative sandwiches, mixing foods that would not normally go together. For example, cheese, jam, custard and gravy. This activity helps children to think about usual food combinations as well as allowing them the fun of being creative with foods. Draw or paint pictures of the sandwiches. You could even try making some of the sandwiches.

### Decorating biscuits

Use small tubes of writing icing, silver balls, sugar flowers and any other edible bits and pieces to decorate home-made or bought biscuits. Show the children how to squeeze out the icing and use it to stick decorations onto their biscuit. This is a gloriously messy and creative activity. You do need to supervise carefully to discourage the children from eating all the decorations and to help with tiny items such as silver balls. The materials are also rather expensive - save it for a special treat.

## Touch games

Try the following games with the children to focus on their sense of touch. They can be adapted for use with different ages and older ones can be encouraged to talk about their reactions to the different textures.

The activities link with the same Stepping Stones as the 'Taste games', also:

- ❑ Begin to describe the texture of things.

### A feely bag

Gather a few familiar objects such as a toy car, a spoon, a plastic cup, a book, a pencil. Let the children feel the objects, showing them how to explore as thoroughly as possible with their hands and fingers - cupping objects in the palm of the hand, touching points and angles with a finger tip, tracing curves and smooth surfaces, rubbing between the thumb and fingers. Use texture words (rough, bumpy, smooth, crinkly, crumpled, scratchy) to describe the surfaces of the objects. Make sure that the children can name each object before placing it in a drawstring bag. Invite a child to reach into the bag with both hands, choose an object, feel it, then name it. Alternatively, you can name an object and ask her to find it.

If you can find identical pairs of objects, a third option is to give the child an object to feel and then ask her to find its matching pair in the bag through touch alone.

Make these activities easier by putting just two or three contrasting objects in the bag.

### A shape feely bag

Once your children know the names of shapes and solids, make up a drawstring bag with a number of shapes inside. Solid shapes are easier to recognise through touch alone, but you can also try plane (flat) shapes with children who have done a lot of touch and shape work.

Follow the same pattern of activities as the ordinary feely bag: choosing a shape to feel and identify, searching for a named shape and finding a shape pair. Make the activities easier by putting just two or three contrasting shapes in the bag - a sphere and a cube rather than a cube and a cuboid. If you do not have solid shape sets in your setting, look out for alternatives such as balls for spheres, wooden bricks for cubes and cuboids and Smartie tubes for cylinders.

### Texture pairs

Make up texture pairs by gluing different substances onto thick card. Velvet, sandpaper, wood, split dried peas, cotton wool and straw are all substances with interesting textures.

Younger children can feel the cards and match them by looking and feeling. Older children can try matching by touch alone. Ask the child to shut her eyes or wear a blindfold. Give her one card to feel then let her feel some more, including the pair of the first card. Is she able to find the matching texture?

ACTIVITY

Use texture words to describe the cards: soft (velvet); rough (sandpaper); bumpy (dried peas); fluffy (cotton wool); ridged (straw).

### Temperature pairs

Fill pairs of plastic bottles with hot water, warm water and cold water. Show the child how to feel each bottle by wrapping her whole hand around its body. Introduce the words hot, cold and warm.

Older children can try matching the bottles by touch alone. Give a child one bottle to feel then let her feel the others, including the pair for the first bottle. Is she able to find the matching temperature? You can also see how well the children can hold the sensory memory of a temperature over a period of time. Set out one of each pair (hot, cold and warm) at the far end of the room. Position yourself at the opposite end of the room with a small group and the other three bottles. Give a child one of the bottles to feel and then ask her to leave it behind and go and find its match.

### Sorting through touch

Gather a collection of soft objects and a collection of hard objects, such as cotton wool, a small cushion, a teddy, a velvet hair band, a mitten; a pebble, a spoon, a small tea tray, a wooden brick, a book. Show the children how to sort the objects into two groups - hard and soft. Older children can search for objects in the setting that can then be added to the 'soft' and the 'hard' groups.

## Smelling games

Try the following games with the children to focus on their sense of smell. They can be adapted for use with different ages and older ones can be encouraged to talk about their reactions to the different smells. Choose substances carefully. Avoid any substance that is not meant to be smelled (cleaning materials, for example). Don't include anything that smells too strong or unpleasant and be aware that some smells may adversely affect children with asthma and allergies.

The activities link with the same Stepping Stones as the 'Taste games'.

### Smelling substances

Prepare a number of familiar substances with recognisable smells. Toothpaste, orange segments, soap - anything that your children are familiar with. Ask the children to smell them. Do they like the smell? What does it make them think of? Encourage the children to respond to the smells with facial expressions. Smells are perhaps the hardest non-visual experiences to describe in language but there are some words you can introduce - sickly, sharp, sweet and floral can all be applied to odours. You can also use qualitative language: 'It smells delicious/disgusting' puts into language your own reaction to a smell. Use vocal and facial expression to help the children understand the meaning of your words.

### Smelling pairs

Put substances into yoghurt pots with holes punched in the lids. Choose solid substances such as a piece of lemon, or drip liquids onto cotton wool. Can the children guess what the smells are?

If you make up pairs of smells, older children can try to match them through smell alone. Choose substances with contrasting smells - chocolate sauce and lemon juice rather than lemon juice and orange juice.

### Tasting without smell

Demonstrate to the children that the sense of smell affects our ability to taste. Start off by showing the children how to hold their noses. Give them something to sniff while holding their noses so they can discover for themselves how this blocks off the ability to smell. Give them a piece of food to taste while holding their noses, then let them try the food normally. Talk about the differences in taste experience.

## Using a blindfold

Many of these activities suggest using a blindfold to 'cut off' the child's visual sense and make it easier for her to focus on touch, taste or smell. Always bear in mind that children need to feel secure in their surroundings before they will happily accept a blindfold. Some children may never want to use it. Don't push the child; shutting eyes or looking away can be substituted, and it really doesn't matter if the child peeps. Keep these activities light-hearted.

If you do use blindfolds, make sure you have a separate one for each child or place a fresh, folded tissue inside to maintain hygiene.

## Touch and smell journeys

Once you have tried a few activities to focus on the sense of touch, take your children on a journey around the setting, searching for different textures in the environment. For example, the smooth, shiny cold taps in the toilets, the soft, squidgy cushions in the book corner, the bumpy Stickle bricks, the rough, grainy step by the back door, the ridged, rough bark on the tree. Introduce the names of substances and textures as you go along.

You can do exactly the same with smells. Try the soap in the cloakroom, the herbs growing in the garden, the playdough, the clay, the pencils, the fish food. If necessary, plant a few 'smelly' items in your setting. As with textures, introduce the names of substances and words to describe smells as you go along.

**Assessment**

❑ In the first instance, the children need to become aware of the different senses. Look out for signs of understanding that we use the nose for smelling, the tongue and mouth for tasting and the hands and fingers for feeling.

❑ How expressively can the child communicate her sensory likes and dislikes with language, facial expressions and gestures? How well does she retain and use different taste, smell and texture words? Texture and taste are useful for making comparisons. Look out for whether the child can distinguish between qualities such as hard and soft or salt and sweet.

❑ Touch and smell journeys can demonstrate how readily older children use their senses in exploring their environment. Are they able to find substances with interesting smells or textures? If you make maps, look out for how well the children can recall the textures and smells they experienced on their journey.

Encourage the children to make their own choices about what to touch or smell.

If you plan to create touch and smell maps with your older children (see below), make notes of the discoveries made on your journeys.

## Touch and smell maps

This is a demanding activity, designed to stretch older children. It requires them to remember the different texture or smell discoveries they made on their journey and recreate the order of the journey on a map. Making the map itself uses art and craft skills such as drawing, colouring and cutting out.

The activity links with the following Stepping Stones:

❑ Show an interest in what they see ... smell, touch and feel/Further explore an experience using a range of senses.

❑ Use body language, gestures, facial expression or words to indicate personal satisfaction or frustration.

❑ Make comparisons.

❑ Try to capture experiences and responses with ... paint or other materials and words.

❑ Begin to describe the texture of things.

### What you will need

A large piece of paper; small pieces of paper; pencils and coloured pencils; a brightly coloured wax crayon; scissors; Blu-tak.

### Getting ready

Remind yourself of the journey you took - where you started from and the direction in which you travelled around the setting. This is important in making your map. Unless you can remember the different things and the order in which you experienced them, check the notes you made during your journey.

### What to do

Keep the group small so that each child can be as involved as possible in the activity. Talk about the journey with the children and go through all the different things you smelled or touched. Ask the children to draw and cut out little pictures of the different objects. You will also need a picture of the place where you started and ended your journey. If a child finishes her picture before the others, ask her to make a drawing of your starting point, for example, the carpet area.

Spread out the large piece of paper. Remind the children that you set out on your journey from the carpet area and ask the child who drew the picture to Blu-tak it to the top of the paper. Ask the children if they can remember the first thing you felt - for example, the cushions. Prompt them if necessary. Can the children remember what the cushions felt like? Ask the child who has drawn the cushions to Blu-tak her picture to the paper. Show her how to position it below and to one side of the carpet picture. Once you have the starting point and the first object attached to the paper, you can show the children how to draw a red line between the two. Explain that the line shows you walking from the carpet to the bookcase.

Continue until all the texture objects have been attached to the map, working around the paper so that your red line ends up back at the carpet where you started from.

You can make the map as simple or as complex as you wish. You can include just a few of the objects you felt, or you can include lots, depending on how long your group maintain their interest in the activity.

Once your map is finished, talk about how to word a heading with the children. For example: 'These are the things we felt on our journey around the room'. You can also add labels for the objects and the textures: the smooth bookcase; the rough stone step; the cold shiny tap. If you have any children who are starting to write, ask them to help you make the labels.

Display the map in your setting and encourage the children to look at it and retrace their touch or smell journey. This is important in helping the children realise the purpose of maps.

Creative Development

# Making up stories

Storytelling is great fun and gives the child the opportunity to organise her thoughts into a logical sequence as well as use language to express her ideas. Storytelling also gives the children the chance to explore how a story is constructed, particularly if you help your group to include story elements such as a main character, a sequence of events and an ending. Once you have made up your story, you can act it out with props and dressing-up clothes, puppets or story boards.

## Making up a story

This activity involves the children in making up a group story. You can give them as much or as little direction as needed, depending on their age and previous storytelling experience. Your main role is to get them started, help them to keep to a story format and encourage a contribution from all the children in the group.

As the story progresses, you can write it down in front of the children. This helps to demonstrate the link between writing and stories.

The activity links with the following Stepping Stones:

❑ Enjoy stories based on themselves and people and places they know well/ Introduce a story line or narrative into their play/Play co-operatively as part of a group to act out a narrative.

❑ Describe experiences and past actions/Try to capture experiences and responses with ... words.

**What you will need**

A clipboard, paper and pen or pencil for writing down the children's ideas.

**Getting ready**

Plan some story themes to suggest to the children. Choose topics that are familiar to the children - a recent trip, a special event or a favourite book will each give the children plenty of experiences to draw from. Plan the make-up of your group. Keep numbers as small as possible and try to include one or two who will make lots of contribution and provide a lead for the younger or quieter children.

**What to do**

Once you have explained that you are all going to make up a story together, the first step is to choose your story theme. You can either offer your suggestions for the children to choose from or ask for ideas from the group. Explain to the children that you are deciding what your story will be about.

The next step is to choose who the story will be about - the main character or characters. Decide on names for the characters.

The third step is to decide where the story takes place - the setting. Again, you can talk about this but keep the discussion linked to the story theme.

Make a written note of what the story is about, who it is about and where it happens. This can be a useful reminder if you want to carry on or develop the story in a later session.

You can now get on with making up the story. Lead the children through the events, asking questions and prompting if necessary. If your story is based on an experience the children have had, draw out their memories of what happened. Encourage them to use sensory memories. What did something look like, feel like, sound like? Help them to bring their feelings into the story by talking about their emotional reaction to a particular event or incident.

Be as flexible as possible. Your role is to help the group maintain a basic story structure, such as sticking to the same main characters and prompting with 'What happened next?' questions; leave the children free to develop the content in their own way.

The final step is to decide when the story needs to be drawn to a close and to help the children to come up with an appropriate ending. The emotional element of an ending is important. Talk about whether you want it to be happy or sad. Try to add an ending that is meaningful for this age group, such as going back home, having tea

**Early Learning Goals**

These activities will help you work towards the following goals:

❑ Express and communicate ideas, thoughts and feelings by using ... imaginative and role play (and) movement.

❑ Use their imagination in ... imaginative and role play and stories.

❑ Respond in a variety of ways to what they see, touch and feel.

and going to bed or waving goodbye to someone in the story.

As you progress, make a written note of the events of the story so that it can be told again at a later stage.

Your very youngest children may not be ready for the storytelling part of the activity although they can join in with making story board figures. They can also sit and listen to the final story or watch as it is acted out.

Encourage younger ones and less verbal children to join in with making up the story as much as they are able. Ask simple questions to help them come up with ideas and remember that the experience of listening to the discussion and being part of the group is as important as making lots of contribution.

Older children and those with a well developed imagination will play a pivotal part in developing the story. These children also need to learn that others in the group must have a chance to contribute.

Once your story is finished, the children can act it out with dressing-up clothes, story props or puppets. Encourage the children to decide for themselves what props they will need.

## making a story board

A story board enables the children to use art and craft skills to create their own storytelling props. These can then be used to act out and make up stories.

The activity links with the following Stepping Stones:

❑ Use ideas involving filling, overlapping ...

❑ Work creatively on a small or large scale.

### Assessment

❑ Making up stories involves three main aspects:

- the ability to put ideas into words
- using the imagination
- introducing story elements such as main characters and endings

Make a note of how well your children can draw on each of these skills and how much you have to prompt them. Look out also for times when the children introduce spontaneous narrative into their play. Provide a tape recorder and encourage children to record their own stories. This is a good way of assessing how their storytelling skills are progressing.

❑ When making story board figures, observe how creatively the children make them. Are the older ones starting to select suitable colours and substances to match the character?

❑ Observe the children playing with the figures. Do they use them to create a story line? How logically does the story link with the story board characters?

❑ Show an interest in what they touch and feel/Further explore an experience using a range of senses.

❑ Pretend that one object represents another, especially when objects have characteristics in common.

❑ Use available resources to create props to support role play.

❑ Introduce a story line or narrative into their play/Play co-operatively as part of a group to act out a narrative.

### What you will need

Scraps of felt; wool, lace, sequins, feathers (optional); templates of figures; scissors; PVA glue, pots and glue spatulas; a thin wooden board or heavy duty cardboard; a piece of felt large enough to cover the board; Velcro hooks; needle and thread.

### Getting ready

Depending on the age and previous experience of your children, decide on how much advance preparation you need to do. Compile a list of the figures you want to make. Choose appropriate substances to decorate the felt.

Cut the board and the large piece of felt to size. Make sure the felt is larger than the board so that you can fold it over the edges. Glue the felt firmly to the board.

### What to do

Show the children how to cut out and glue together pieces of felt to make story figures. Encourage them to choose appropriate bits and pieces to decorate their figures. Once the children have finished their creations, they need to be made strong enough to survive being played with. Add a few stitches to each detail so that they are sewn as well as glued together. Cut out a shape from felt to mirror the shape of the child's figure and sew on a piece of hooked Velcro. Glue the shape firmly to the back of the character, to hide your stitches. If you have started to do simple sewing with your older ones, they may be able to help with stitching the details.

Show the children how to press the character onto the board so that the Velcro hooks attach to the felt. Leave them to play freely with their characters. Emphasise that the characters are delicate and must be handled carefully. Keep an eye on them and make any repairs as necessary. Be ready to withdraw a figure from use if a child's work is starting to disintegrate.

# Weather music

Music and dance have all kinds of representational and communicative possibilities. Many pre-school children are ready to connect a piece of music with a particular idea and even the youngest can dance or play musical instruments to connect with whatever theme you are looking at.

These activities are based on the theme of seasonal weather, such as summer thunderstorms, winter snow, spring showers and autumn winds. They follow the pattern of listening to music, moving to music and choosing and playing instruments to represent the different weathers.

**Early Learning Goals**

These activities will help you work towards the following goals:

❑ Recognise and explore how sounds can be changed, sing simple songs from memory, recognise repeated sounds and sound patterns.

❑ Express and communicate ideas, thoughts and feelings by using ... a variety of songs and musical instruments.

❑ Respond in a variety of ways to what they ... hear.

❑ Use imagination in ... music.

## Listening to weather music

Introduce the idea of linking music with a theme by listening to some carefully chosen recordings. Select the music to link with the season you are looking at.

The activity links with the following Stepping Stones:

❑ Try to capture experiences and responses with music ...

❑ Begin to use representation as a means of communication.

### What you will need

Tapes or CDs of music to represent seasonal weather; pictures or artefacts linked with the weather; a CD player or tape recorder; cushions or mats.

### Getting ready

Choose one or two weathers that link with the current season. Ensure that the children have had recent experience of the weather - younger children may not remember snow during the summer months, particularly if you live in a part of the country where snow is rare. Having chosen your weathers, pick some appropriate music. If possible, include a variety of musical styles (classical, jazz, folk). For example, passages from Grieg's *Peer Gynt* or some of Holst's *Planet Suite* would work well for wind or thunder; Gershwin's *Rhapsody in Blue* suggests a hot, sunny day when everyone is feeling too lazy to move; try Vivaldi's *Four Seasons* to cover all weathers, or Mike Oldfield's *Tubular Bells* for the sound of gentle spring rain or snow.

Put out the cushions in a quiet corner of the setting, making the area as comfortable as possible. Choose a time of day when the children are alert but settled.

### What to do

Settle the children comfortably on the cushions or mats. Talk about the appropriate weather, for example, a spring shower. What does it look like, feel like, sound like? Focus on elements that are meaningful to this age group - wearing rainy weather clothes and wellies, splashing in puddles, not being able to go out to play in the garden.

Explain to the children that you are all going to listen to some music. Encourage them to sit as quietly and as still as possible and to shut their eyes.

Play the music for a couple of minutes. Stop playing as soon as the group gets restless.

Concentrate on helping the younger ones to sit quietly with eyes closed and listen to the music. Point out the cassette recorder or CD player and help them discover that the music is coming from the machine.

Talk about the music with the older ones. Did they like it? How did it make them feel? What did they think about when they were listening? Explain to the children that the music made you think about a shower of rain - but take this opportunity to emphasise that response to music is a personal thing.

If the children are settled, play the music again.

## Moving to weather music

Introduce the idea of linking music with a theme by moving and dancing to some carefully chosen recordings.

movements along with the music.

Leave younger ones to move freely to the music. The idea of music representing something else is a sophisticated concept that your little ones will not be ready for. At this stage, simply concentrate on dancing along to the music and enjoying the activity.

Older ones can develop the idea of music 'reminding' them of something else and can tailor their movements to express particular ideas. Match your own movements to the rhythm of the music to encourage them to move in time with the music.

Some other weather related movements to try:

❑ tiptoeing like the gentle spring rain;

❑ stomping about like a rain storm;

❑ rubbing arms, stamping feet and shaking and shivering to get warm;

❑ playing in the snow, throwing snowballs;

❑ wiping foreheads, sighing and flopping down in the heat.

Select the music to link with the season you are looking at.

This activity contributes to the following Stepping Stones:

❑ Try to capture experiences and responses with music (and) dance ...

❑ Respond to sound with body movement.

❑ Imitate and create movement in response to music.

❑ Begin to use representation as a means of communication.

**What you will need**

Tapes or CDs of music to represent seasonal weather; a CD player or tape recorder.

**What to do**

Explain to the children that you are going to dance to the music you listened to earlier. Talk about movements that link with the weather. Imagine you are out in the rain - what do you do? (splash in the puddles, cover your head with your hands, dance in the rain, run to get home...) Try one or two of the movements then play the rainy music and perform the

## Making weather sounds

Along with listening and moving to appropriate music, the children can also use percussion instruments to represent a theme. Seasonal weather makes a good starting point because much of it includes sound. Rain (a

gentle shower or heavy downpour), thunder and wind are all easy to link with percussion sounds. For older ones who are ready, you can introduce the more abstract idea of sounds representing softly falling snow or a sultry hot day.

This activity links with the following Stepping Stones:

❑ Show an interest in the way musical instruments sound/Explore the different sounds of instruments.

❑ Try to capture experiences and responses with music (and) dance ...

❑ Begin to use representation as a means of communication.

❑ Make comparisons.

### What you will need

A range of percussion instruments - drums, cymbals, triangles, castanets, shakers, tambourines, rhythm sticks; pictures and items associated with the weathers you are planning to play.

### Getting ready

Choose weather that links with the current season, as with 'Listening to weather music' and 'Moving to weather music'. If possible, choose two contrasting weathers, such as a gentle shower of rain and a thunderstorm.

### What to do

Talk about the gentle shower of rain and the thunderstorm, focussing in particular on their different sounds. Work through the percussion instruments with the children, asking a different child to play each instrument. Decide whether it sounds like rain or thunder, encouraging the children to express their own thoughts and ideas. Introduce appropriate words as you go along - the triangle sounds like drizzle, the shakers sound like a shower if you shake them gently, the drums boom like thunder, the cymbals crash like thunder.

Divide the instruments into two groups and distribute them among the children. Keep the gentle rain instruments on one side and the booming thunder instruments on the other side. Allow the children to play with their instruments and practise making their sounds.

Explain to the children that you are going to use the instruments to make sounds like a rain shower and a thunderstorm. Adapt the activity to suit the age and previous experience of the children:

Let younger ones simply explore and discover how to get sound from their instruments. Asking them to play separately (either as individuals or in two groups) will also help them learn to listen to instructions such as when to start playing and when to stop playing.

Older ones can be encouraged to play their rain instruments quietly and then get louder and louder as the rain gets heavier and heavier. The thunder players can watch for your signal to start playing and stop playing. They can also make louder and quieter crashes of thunder. Explain to them that you are the conductor and they must watch you carefully for instructions.

Other weather combinations you can try:

❑ A gentle breeze blowing fallen leaves/a howling gale making the trees thrash (link with autumn).

❑ Hot sunny weather that makes you feel lazy/a thunderstorm with heavy rain or thunder (link with summer).

❑ Gentle snow/pouring rain or wind (link with winter).

❑ Gentle rain shower/heavy rain shower (link with spring).

Look out also for unusual weathers that occur while the children are with you - a hail storm, flashes of lightning, sunshine and showers creating a rainbow. Follow up these experiences as soon as possible by using the percussion instruments to represent the different weathers.

## Other activities

❑ Link the weather music with appropriate dressing-up clothes. Gather cagoules, sou'westers, wellies and small umbrellas; T-shirts, sun hats, flip-flops and sunglasses; woolly hats, scarves and mittens. Ask children to bring in their own, if necessary. Talk about the different clothing, how it feels, what it is made of and why we wear it. Encourage the children to choose and try on the relevant clothing. Dressing-up helps the children with dancing and moving to weather music. After the activity, make the dressing-up clothes freely available in your setting.

❑ Try using home-made percussion instruments to represent weather sounds (see 'Making musical instruments' pages 46-49).

❑ Try using body percussion sounds to represent the weather. Stamp feet or drum fists on the floor to represent heavy rain; clap hands and punch palms with fists to make claps of thunder; tap fingers on head to represent snowfall or gentle rain. You can also make voice sounds - shhhing for rain, howling for wind, sighing for hot weather.

❑ Choose other themes for music and movement. Animals, vehicles, emotions, physical states such as feeling sleepy or energetic all work well when set to carefully chosen music. Try to follow the pattern of combining two contrasting themes - a mouse and an elephant; a bicycle and a plane; feeling happy, feeling angry.

❑ Use paint and collage materials to make weather pictures. Choose hot colours for summer (reds, yellows, oranges) and cold colours for winter (pale green, pale blue, white, grey). Make swirly patterns with a paint brush to suggest wind and stormy rain. Use watered down paint to make rainy pictures.

### Assessment

❑ Observe the children as they listen to the music and make a note of how absorbed they appear to be. Bear in mind that fidgeting does not necessarily mean that a child is not listening or enjoying the experience.

❑ How do older children respond to talking about the music once it is finished?

❑ Dance involves moving in time to the rhythm of the music and expressing ideas through movement. Look out for how well the child can co-ordinate her body as she moves. How well is she able to express certain ideas, feelings and experiences through dance? Is she able to adapt her movements to changes in the music, such as fast to slow or loud to quiet?

❑ Look out for whether younger ones can hold their instruments correctly. Are they then able to produce sounds from their instruments and respond to instructions to start playing and stop playing? Can older ones control the loudness/quietness of the sounds they produce and are they able to link an instrument with a particular weather? The ability to do this is an indicator of whether or not the child is starting to grasp the idea of music as a form of communication.

**Creative Development**

## Water

# Miming

Miming is a special kind of acting in that it requires the children to express an event or action using only movement and gestures. At this early stage, the mime needs to be centred around everyday, familiar activities.

Turning the mime into a guessing game adds an extra challenge to the mimer and helps to engage the rest of the group. Linking the mime with photographs makes the guessing easier by giving the children clues. You can base your mimes around any theme. Activities related to water give a wide choice of everyday actions and provide something for all ages.

## Water miming

This activity links different mimes with photographs. You can collect pictures from books or drawings but there are a number of advantages to using your own photos:

❑ your own photographs will link directly with the mime;

❑ posing for the photos gives the children a little practice run for the mime itself;

❑ the children have the added interest of seeing themselves in the picture.

The activity links with the following Stepping Stones:

❑ Develop a repertoire of actions by putting a sequence of movements together.

❑ Begin to use representation as a means of communication.

**Early Learning Goals**

These activities will help you work towards the following goals:

❑ Express and communicate ideas, thoughts and feelings by using ... imaginative and role play (and) movement.

❑ Respond in a variety of ways to what they see, touch and feel.

### What you will need

A set of photographs showing the children engaged in everyday, water-based activities.

### Getting ready

Make a list of water based activities. Ask the children for their suggestions:

❑ washing hands

❑ washing face

❑ cleaning teeth

❑ drinking

❑ rinsing paint brush in water

❑ splashing in puddles

❑ playing in the paddling pool

❑ swimming (for older ones)

❑ putting up an umbrella (for older ones)

❑ rowing (for older ones)

Take photographs of the children engaged in as many of the activities as you can. If possible, have them developed in a large format.

### What to do

Show the children the photographs of the water-based activities and talk about them. Who is in each picture? What is happening in the pictures? Show the children your camera and ask them if they remember you taking the pictures. This will help them to connect the camera with the photograph.

Choose one of the pictures and ask a child to mime the action. Emphasise that you are just going to use movements - no words or sounds. Explain to the children that this special kind of acting is called mime. If necessary, do a mime yourself first, or ask a helper to start off the session. If you want to keep the group as active as possible, all the children can do a mime at the same time. You or a helper can take the lead at the front of the group.

Vary the actions you select to suit the age and developmental level of the children.

Younger children can try drinking or washing their faces. If necessary mime alongside them so that they can imitate your movements. Getting used to participating and performing within a group is an important aim of this activity for little ones.

Older ones can try more challenging mimes, such as washing hands, rinsing paint brushes or putting up an umbrella. Encourage them to use their own ideas to develop the mime: washing hands can include putting in the plug, turning on the taps, remembering to turn the taps off, and so on.

## Guess the mime

This activity introduces the extra

challenge of guessing the mime. To begin with, the children are given clues by choosing which of two photographs the child is miming. Extend the choice as the children's miming and guessing abilities develop. Keep the group as small as possible for this activity, to enable each child to have plenty of turns.

'Guess the mime' links with the same Stepping Stones as the previous activity.

**What you will need**
A set of water activity photographs.

**What to do**
Choose two photographs with contrasting activities, such as washing hands and splashing in puddles. Show the children the photographs and talk about them. Ask a child to come to the front. Explain to the group that the child is going to mime one of the activities for them to guess.

Show the child one of the photographs, without the rest of the group seeing which one. It adds to the fun of the activity if you make a big secret of this. The child then mimes the activity and the rest of the group try to guess which one they are miming. If necessary, keep the two photographs on display to jog memories.

## Match the mime

This activity gives the children a wider choice of mimes to guess. It also enables the mimer to choose her own mime rather than being directed by the adult. Play it with older ones or when the children have had plenty of practice with all the different mimes.

'Match the mime' links with the same Stepping Stones as the previous activities.

**Assessment**

❑ Look out for signs that the children have grasped the concept of using movement and gesture to express an action. How successfully can they communicate with their audience?

❑ To what extent can they draw on their own experiences, both in discussion before the activity and during the mime itself? How far does each child develop her performance?

❑ Observe the audience to see how closely each child is concentrating on the mime and to judge whether they have grasped the idea of the mime representing an activity for them to identify.

**What you will need**

The set of water activity photographs.

**What to do**

Put out as many of the photographs as you want to use. Ask a single child or a small group to come to the front and mime one of the activities. Ask one of the audience to pick out the photograph that matches the mime.

Younger ones can be given a limited choice by setting out a small number of photographs showing obvious and contrasting actions (washing hands, splashing in puddles, washing face). Give the children as much support as necessary to do their mime.

Older ones can be given a wide choice of photographs. Include some more complex actions such as putting up an umbrella, and actions that look similar such as cleaning teeth and drinking.

## Videoing mime

If you have access to a camcorder, try making a video of the children's mime. This adds another dimension to the activity as well as introducing the children to video technology. When you have made the recording, the children can watch their performances and try to guess the action being mimed.

## Other activities

❑ Make a wall display with the photographs. Add a label challenging the children to mime the different activities. Put out a basket with a range of water-based props to encourage imaginative and role play - a plastic cup and jug, a hand towel, a child's umbrella, arm bands and swimming rings, wellies and a sou'wester.

❑ Try other mimes. Choose whatever theme you wish or think of some contrasting pairs of actions such as:

- dusting a delicate ornament/ brushing a pair of shoes;

- stroking a rabbit/patting a large dog;

- putting on shoes (laces? buckles? Velcro?)/pulling on mittens or gloves;

- eating an apple/eating spaghetti;

- being an elephant/being a snake.

Wherever possible, give the child the real experience first.

You can follow the same format of taking photos, playing guessing and matching games and videoing mimes. Alternatively, you can save the activity for a quick fill-in at the beginning or end of a session.

What Learning Looks Like... THEME

Creative Development

Colour

# Painting

Paint is one of the most important resources in the early years setting. Its bright colours and satisfying texture make it a firm favourite with most children. It is also extremely versatile when it comes to creating different art and craft effects.

These activities start off with the basic skills of painting for the very youngest children. There are also activities showing the different effects that can be created with paint, activities encouraging younger children to explore colours one at a time and colour mixing for older children.

Your aim with painting should always be:

❑ to help the children develop their basic skills;

❑ to give them lots of opportunity to paint freely so that they can consolidate their skills and express their creativity in their own way.

Try to avoid projects where you end up with 20 identical pieces of work. The 'Painting pebbles' activity allows for individual expression within a planned structure. It can also be adapted to suit all age groups.

This activity links with the following Stepping Stones:

❑ Begin to differentiate colours.

❑ Differentiate marks and movements on paper.

❑ Use lines to enclose a space, then begin to use these shapes to represent objects.

❑ Make ... paintings.

❑ Work creatively on a large or small scale.

❑ Respond to comments and questions, entering into dialogue about their creations.

**Early Learning Goals**

These activities will help you work towards the following goals:

❑ Explore colour, shape, texture, form and space in two dimensions.

❑ Express and communicate ideas, thoughts and feelings by using a widening range of materials and suitable tools.

❑ Use imagination in art and design.

❑ Respond in a variety of ways to what they see, touch and feel.

## Using the painting easel

The aim with this activity is to introduce all the practical skills the child needs in order to use the painting easel independently. She can then be left to paint as and when she wants - the best way of enabling her to express her imagination through paint.

### What you will need

An easel; non-spill pots of paint in two or three colours; thick brushes; a supply of paper; a painting apron; a rack to hang paintings to dry.

### Getting ready

Place the easel in a corner of your setting. If possible, keep it permanently set up so that children can paint whenever they wish. If you have a double-sided easel, two children can paint at a time. Plan where to keep painting paper so that children can access it easily, where to hang the apron and where the children can place their finished paintings (a rack for drying clothes works well.)

### What to do

Show the children how to put on the apron, where to find the paper, how to clip it to the easel and where to put the finished painting to dry. Emphasise the importance of asking an adult to write names on paintings so that the right painting can be taken home at the end of the day.

Introduce skills such as wiping the paint brush against the opening of the pot so that the brush is not overloaded with paint. Highlight to the children that each brush should go back in its pot. Colour coding brushes can be useful - a blue-handled brush for the blue paint and so on. Keep an eye on this and remind the children not to mix up the brushes.

Once the children have established these practical routines, leave them to paint freely. If you have problems with a long queue of children, invest in more easels or make a list of names so that everyone gets their turn. Do,

however, let the children watch each other paint. The painting easel can be a very sociable experience and the children can inspire each other with their different ideas and approaches.

## Painting techniques

Once children have had plenty of opportunity to explore the paint freely, you can start introducing a variety of different paint techniques.

### What you will need

Thick brushes and thin brushes; paint; paper; water pots, pipettes or spoons; flour; thick card cut with notches.

### What to do

Choose from the following techniques:

❑ Use an old, thick brush. Show the children how to load the brush with paint and stab downwards on the paper to create a stippled effect. Leave to dry and then go over the top with a different colour.

❑ Load a thick brush with paint and press down along the side of the bristles to create a fan effect. Encourage older ones to create patterns, alternating different colours and varying the space between the fans.

❑ Show the children how to load the paint brush with paint and then paint until the brush is almost dry. Encourage older ones to compare the results and point out that you can start to see the brush strokes as the paint becomes used up.

❑ Mix paint with wallpaper paste or flour to make it very thick and mix another lot with water to make it very thin. Use both types of paint and compare the results. Cut notches in thick card and comb patterns into the thick paint. Create patterns in the watery paint by blowing with a straw (do this flat on a table rather than at the easel).

❑ Pour a teaspoonful or pipette of water onto paper and drop blobs of paint onto the water. Try using two different colours. Leave to dry (do this flat on a table rather than at the easel).

❑ Show the children how to cover a complete area of paper with paint brush strokes, working horizontally or vertically. This activity introduces the idea of painting a specified area and controlling your brush strokes, rather than using the paint randomly.

❑ Show the children how to paint an outline. Leave it to dry before painting in the inside, so that the paint does not run.

Remind the children to use these different techniques in their free, individual painting at the easel. If painting with flour-thickened paint or watered-down paint appeals to your children, try to make these materials available at all times so that the children can use them whenever they wish. If you need to prevent younger children from gaining access to them, explain to your older ones that they can come and ask you for them whenever they want to use them.

## Exploring colours

This activity is suitable for all age groups. Leave the children to respond to the materials at whatever level of skill they have reached.

The activity links with the same Stepping Stones as 'Using the painting easel'.

### What you will need

One colour in two or three shades; thick brushes; sugar paper in the same colour as the paint.

### Getting ready

Select the colour paint you want to use and mix it to create two or three shades. If you are using one of the three primary colours (red, yellow or blue) you can darken or lighten by adding black or white. Only a small amount of black is needed to darken a colour quite noticeably. If you are using one of the secondary colours (green, orange, purple) you could add one of its two constituent primaries. For example, if you add blue or yellow to green you will get a lighter yellowy green or a darker bluey green.

Make sure that you also provide sugar paper in the same colour as the paint, but do check that the paint shows up. If you have dark green sugar paper, provide two lighter shades of green.

Plan whether you want to introduce a second or third colour, or whether you want to have different children using different colours within the same group and mix up your paint accordingly.

### What to do

Leave your children to paint freely with the two different shades. Use the colour name as much as possible during the activity. If your children can name the colours with confidence, they may be ready for you to introduce the terms 'dark green' and 'light green'. Give the children a second colour and piece of sugar paper if you wish to extend the activity.

### Make a display

The combination of shades on similar coloured paper is surprisingly effective and makes an eye-catching display:

- ❑ Try placing the paintings side by side on the wall like a tiled floor. This looks particularly good if you have two or three different colours that you can alternate, although you do need to make sure that the sugar paper is all the same size.

- ❑ Use the paintings as mounts for more detailed pictures or other work on colour.

- ❑ Develop the activity into a cutting and sticking exercise. When the paintings are dry, ask the children to cut them into small pieces. These can then be stuck onto a contrasting piece of sugar paper to create a colourful collage.

## Mixing colours

Mixing colours with paint involves good hand control and the ability to cope with quite a complex process. Once the child is able to mix her own colours, it widens the options open to her in painting. It also lays the foundations for a much deeper understanding of colour and how it is made up.

This activity links with the same Stepping Stones as 'Using the painting easel', plus:

- ❑ Explore what happens when they mix colours.

### What you will need

Paint in the three primary colours - red, yellow and blue plus black and white; a selection of paint brushes; a water jar; a mixing palette or white plate; white or pale coloured paper.

### Getting ready

Decide which colour mixing technique you want to use and try it out yourself before introducing it to the children. There are two main approaches:

- ❑ Provide a brush for each colour, preferably with matching coloured handle, and an extra brush for mixing. Put a blob of each colour on the palette and then mix using the special mixing brush.

- ❑ Provide just one brush which has to be washed in the water jar after every use, to prevent the colours getting mixed up.

Try some or all of the following colour combinations:

red + blue = purple

red + yellow = orange

blue + yellow = green

red + blue + yellow = brown

red + white = pink

black + white = grey

When mixing purple, green, brown or grey, make sure that you use less blue or black and more yellow or red. Any mixture using yellow will need more yellow than the other colour in the combination. A true purple is difficult to get. If you use a children's paint supplier with a wide range of colours, ask them to recommend the red, yellow and blue that are best for colour mixing.

### What to do

Introduce the activity to the children, explaining that you are going to mix two colours together to make a new colour.

Show the children the technique you have planned in advance, emphasising the importance of not mixing up the brushes or washing the brush thoroughly, depending on which approach you are using.

If the children cope well with the technique for mixing one colour, lead them on to mixing other colours. If they know their colours well, encourage them to guess what new colour they might make. You can also show them how to lighten colours by adding white and darken colours by adding a tiny amount of black.

Encourage the children to use colour mixing in their free painting. Mixed colours can be used to paint rainbows, trees, flowers, colourful traffic jams - wherever the child's imagination takes her. Older children with good hand control can be shown how to add a little more yellow each time to blue or red to create different shades of green or orange. Each shade can be painted onto the paper in a stripe, progressing from dark to light. The same can be done by adding a little white each time to a colour.

## Painting pebbles

This is a simple activity suitable for all ages. The end result is a paperweight or doorstop that can be taken home as a present for Father's Day.

The activity links with the same Stepping Stones as 'Using the painting easel', plus:

❑ Choose particular colours to use for a purpose.

### What you will need

Pebbles or stones; thick paint in three or four colours (finger paint is a good thickness; metallic paint, glitter paint or fluorescent colours are all effective if you want to add variations); cotton wool buds or small pieces of sponge; pieces of felt; high gloss wood or craft varnish.

### Getting ready

Gather your pebbles or stones. Check that you are not breaking any bye-laws if you collect pebbles from beaches. Pebbles give a lovely smooth surface but stones and chunks of rock collected from your own garden can be just as effective. Cut the felt pieces to the same size as the stones or draw shapes on the felt for the children to cut out for themselves. Put the paint in shallow containers with cotton wool buds or sponge pieces.

### What to do

Show the children how to blob the paint onto the pebble. Using cotton wool buds or sponge rather than a paint brush discourages little ones from mixing the colours into a muddy mess although they may still need help in keeping the colours separate. Another alternative is to leave each colour to dry before adding the next.

Let the children paint the pebble in whatever way they wish. Older ones could try painting flowers, shapes or patterns of spots, lines, zig-zags and so on. Encourage each child to paint more than one pebble, preferably choosing different sizes as they will look effective when grouped together.

After the children have gone home, varnish the pebbles with high-gloss wood varnish. This is a part of the activity the children cannot help with, unless you choose instead to varnish the pebbles with a solution of PVA glue (see page 32).

Once the varnish is dry the children can glue the felt shapes to the back of their pebbles. Those children who are ready can cut out their own shapes. When the pebble is complete, show the children how it can be used as a paperweight. Any larger stones may be heavy enough for doorstops.

See how many more unusual objects and surfaces you and your children can find to paint on: wooden spoons; paper plates (look at patterns on plates such as Delftware); large, tough pressed leaves; cotton fabric stretched and pinned to a board (fabric paints can be ironed to create a permanent result but ordinary ready-mixed paint also works well).

### Assessment

❑ Observe the children at the painting easel to assess how well they can hold the paint brush and handle the paint.

❑ Look out for the stage at which each child starts to paint deliberate lines, enclosed shapes and representative images.

❑ Paint is a useful medium for assessing whether children can recognise, distinguish and name colours. Does the child understand that new colours can be made by mixing other colours? How well does the older child cope with the organisational process needed to mix colours?

❑ Look out also for the degree of imagination and creativity the child brings to her free painting.

Creative Development

All about me

# Circle dancing

Circle dancing offers a simple dance pattern that can be developed to suit the age and ability level of your group. It also gives you a forum in which to introduce a range of different dance steps. Younger ones in particular are helped by remaining 'attached' to the rest of the group throughout the dance.

Many children's songs can be adapted for use with the circle dance format. The following activities are based on 'Here We Go Round the Mulberry Bush' and 'If You're Happy and You Know It'. The first song gives all ages the opportunity to focus on and perform actions using different body parts. The second song gives older ones the opportunity to focus on different feelings. The two songs can be used in conjunction with the physical and emotional elements of an 'All about me' project.

**Early Learning Goals**

These activities will help you work towards the following goals:

❑ Explore space ... in three dimensions.

❑ Express and communicate ideas, thoughts and feelings by using ... movement.

❑ Match movements to music.

❑ Use their imagination in dance.

## Here We Go Round the Mulberry Bush

This activity contributes to the following Stepping Stones:

❑ Develop a repertoire of actions by putting a sequence of movements together.

❑ Join in favourite songs.

❑ Enjoy joining in with dancing and ring games.

❑ Begin to move rhythmically.

**Getting ready**

Make a list of body parts and corresponding simple actions. For example:

❑ clap our hands

❑ wriggle our fingers

❑ put up our thumbs

❑ stamp our feet

❑ nod our heads

❑ blink with our eyes

❑ smile with our mouths

❑ tap our noses

❑ kick our legs

❑ stroke our hair

Ask the children to name different body parts and think of some movements. Plan a dance format suitable for the age and previous experience of your children. Include any dance movements you want to introduce.

**What to do**

Ask the children to make a circle by joining hands. Sing 'Here We Go Round the Mulberry Bush', walking round in a circle. Encourage the children to take steps in time to the music. You can either keep the dance simple by walking in the same direction or take eight steps to the left as you sing: 'Here we go round the mulberry bush, the mulberry bush, the mulberry bush', then eight steps in the opposite direction as you sing: 'Here we go round the mulberry bush on a cold and frosty morning'.

Adapt your speed to suit the age group. Younger children will need to go slowly, older ones can step more quickly. At the end of the first two lines, stand still to perform your actions: 'This is the way we tap our feet', and so on.

You can then develop the dance in whatever way you wish. For example:

Take four steps to the left (Here we go round the mulberry bush).

Stand still and clap two times (the mulberry bush, the mulberry bush).

Take four steps to the right (Here we go round the mulberry bush).

Shrink the circle by taking three steps forward into the circle or stretch it by taking three steps outward (on a cold and frosty morning).

As your children develop their dancing skills, try introducing some of the following into the circle format:

❑ skipping (for older ones)

❑ walking on the spot

❑ jumping

❑ pointing toes in and out of the circle

❑ heel to toe movements with the foot (for older ones)

❑ kicking into the circle (with reminders to be very careful)

❑ stretching legs out behind

❑ clapping above heads

❑ spreading out and circling arms above heads

With your younger children, concentrate on the basic format of holding hands, moving round in a circle, developing the ability to step in time to the music, all at the same time as singing the song. Older ones can try more complex dances. As they learn different steps, encourage them to plan their own dance routines.

The simple structure of the circle dance makes it easy for the adults in the ring to guide the children. Be prepared to sing slowly to begin with, as the children get to know the routine. Practise as often as the dance holds the children's interest so that they become more fluent and learn the different dance steps and movements.

## If You're Happy and You Know it

This activity can be linked with the theme of 'feelings'. It contributes to the following Stepping Stones:

❑ Develop a repertoire of actions by putting a sequence of movements together.

❑ Join in favourite songs.

❑ Enjoy joining in with dancing and ring games.

❑ Begin to move rhythmically.

❑ Use body language, gestures, facial expression or words to indicate personal satisfaction or frustration.

### Getting ready

Make a list of common emotions and some actions or facial expressions that might go with those movements:

❑ If you're angry and you know it stamp your feet.

❑ If you're sad and you know it wipe your eyes.

❑ If you're excited and you know it jump up and down.

❑ If you're frightened and you know it hide your face.

Plan a circle dance to fit in with the rhythm of 'If You're Happy and You Know It ...'

### What to do

Talk about different feelings. What kinds of things make them feel sad, happy and so on? How do they behave and what do they do when they have these feelings? Try to use the children's own suggestions although it is useful to have your own list to fall back on.

Practise some of the actions and facial expressions and then form a circle, holding hands. Once the circle has been made, loose hands as the song begins with the action - 'If you're happy and you know it clap your hands'. Clap in time to the song and encourage the children to smile and look happy. Then, join hands and sing: 'If you're happy and you know it and you're sure you want to show it', following whatever dance choreography you have planned. For example, take four steps to the left, or two steps into the circle and two back before standing still and loosing hands to sing and clap a final - 'If you're happy and you know it clap your hands'. Alternatively, you can skip around for the remainder of the song.

**Assessment**

❑ Dance involves moving in time to the rhythm of the music, remembering and being able to reproduce dance steps with grace and control. Look out for how well the child can co-ordinate her body to manage all of these elements at once. Does she step lightly or heavily? Demonstrate lightness of step to the children - a heavy tread may be lack of realisation rather than lack of physical control.

❑ Group dance involves a high level of co-operation with the other dancers. Look out for each child's awareness of others in the group and the shared space in which they are all dancing.

❑ Observe free, spontaneous dancing to assess how well the child co-ordinates her movements and whether she remembers and introduces any of the dance steps you have shown her.

Repeat the dance, using whichever emotion and movement you wish. If you want to explore the same emotion in different ways, introduce some other movements:

❑ If you're angry and you know it clench your fists (try clenching fists and moving them up and down);

❑ If you're angry and you know it make a face (try making an angry facial expression).

People who help us

# Making a frieze

Making a wall frieze is a lovely way of involving the whole group in an art activity. The frieze can be planned to suit the different ages of the children in your setting, as well as giving them the opportunity to use a range of art skills. Because this is a group picture, you can keep the activity simple for the younger ones while stretching the older ones with more challenging tasks.

The ideas given below are just suggestions. Vary the art materials you use for your frieze to fit in with what you have already introduced to your children - but aim to work on a large scale and make sure that you include a variety of art techniques and media.

The frieze described in this activity links with the theme of 'People who help us'. Making a frieze contributes to the following Stepping Stones:

❑ Understand that different media can be combined.

❑ Make .. collages, paintings (and) drawings.

❑ Work creatively on a large and small scale.

### What you will need

Books and pictures showing 'people who help us' - police, nurses and doctors, firefighters, lollipop ladies, and so on; a large strip of paper, such as the back of a wallpaper roll (non-pasted); paint and brushes; sponges and other items for printing; fabric, paper and card scraps, wool, buttons, laces; scissors; glue; drawing pencils, wax crayons and chalks; sugar paper and drawing paper; chalk, soft pencils or marker pens for drawing outlines.

### Getting ready

Choose the people that you wish to feature in your frieze, concentrating on figures that the children are familiar with. Gather as many pictorial sources as possible so that the children can study what the figures look like. If possible, include some artefacts such as appropriate hats and caps, a lollipop, a toy fire engine or a toy doctor's kit.

Plan the different art techniques you intend to use and get ready the appropriate materials, including items such as gold paper for stripes and buttons (or real buttons), wool for hair, red paper for the details on a nurse's uniform and so on. The more organised you are with a large group project such as this one, the better. Divide the activity into separate tasks such as sponge printing uniforms, drawing and cutting out hats, adding collage hair and making faces. Plan groups of children for each task, taking into account age and previous experience.

### What to do

Start off by talking to the children about the project, explaining any new or special details such as how you are going to make the body outlines (see below). Emphasise that every child will help. Talk about the different people you plan to include in the frieze. What can the children remember about the clothes and hats they wear? What might the figures be holding? Look at the pictures and any other related artefacts, focussing on the colour and details of clothes and hats.

To create the frieze, try the following format:

**Making the body outline**: ask a child to lie down on a large piece of paper, arms slightly out from the body. Use a marker pen, soft pencil or chalk to draw around the body outline. Some older children may be able to help with this. Have a good look at the outline once it has been drawn. Try to draw around every child in the group who wants to participate, even if you don't need all the body shapes. Point out that you have made people pictures the same size as the children. One or two older ones may be ready to think about the term 'life size'. Cut out the body shape, involving the children as much as possible.

**Colouring in the uniforms**: use a simple printing technique to colour in

**Early Learning Goals**

These activities will help you work towards the following goals:

❑ Explore colour, shape, texture, form and space in two dimensions.

❑ Express and communicate ideas, thoughts and feelings by using a widening range of materials and suitable tools.

❑ Use imagination in art and design.

❑ Respond in a variety of ways to what they see, touch and feel.

the body of your figures. Even the youngest children can sponge print, and it makes a quick, simple way of colouring in a large area. If you want to use a greater variety of prints, try different objects (see pages 24-25 for ideas.) You could use one type of print for the jacket and another for the legs. An alternative is to introduce painting with a large brush - look out for budget price decorating brushes in your local DIY store.

**Decorating the uniforms**: once the foundation colour of the uniforms has dried, you can add texture with collage. Put out the glue and a selection of fabric and/or paper scraps. Encourage the children to sort out appropriate colours to stick onto the uniforms. For example, white scraps for the nurse, dark blue for the police officer, yellow for the firefighter. You may wish to limit this activity by just doing the legs or the jacket for each figure. Little ones can simply glue on the scraps. Older children can use their cutting skills by making their own shapes.

**Adding details to the uniform**: look closely at the pictures you have gathered and name buttons, markings on uniforms, emblems, shoe laces and other details. Provide older children with a range of collage materials - coloured paper, wool, buttons, laces. Encourage them to decide what details they wish to add to each figure and to choose appropriate materials.

**Making the faces**: cut out face shapes from pink paper or get older children to draw and cut out their own. Ask the children to draw faces onto the shapes. As an alternative, the children can cut out shapes from coloured paper to make eyes, mouth and nose. Name the features and help the children to position them on the face. Give older ones a selection of coloured wool and cotton wool to make hair. Show them how to put the glue onto the head and then add the wool. Gluing wool can be quite tricky - be ready to help. Once they are finished, the faces can be stuck onto the head part of the cut-out body shape.

**Making the hats**: give older children real hats (a police helmet, a firefighter's helmet, a nurse's cap, a postal worker's cap), or clear pictures to look at. Show them how to draw a hat that will fit on the head of the cut-out body shape. Paint in the hat with the appropriate colour. Look at the hat details on the picture and choose a technique to create the detail. For example, red strips of paper can be used to make the cross on a nurse's cap; a piece of silver foil or card can be cut into a shape and drawn on with a pencil to create the badge for a police helmet.

**Making the background**: the background can be as simple or as detailed as you wish to make it. The most straightforward approach is to sponge print onto your strip of wallpaper - pale blue at the top to represent sky and pale green at the bottom to represent grass. If you want to carry on, you can then choose an item to link with each character: a zebra crossing made from black and white paint, a big red fire engine painted onto a large sheet of sugar paper and cut out and stuck on to the background.

**Assembling the frieze**: involve the children as much as possible with putting together the frieze. Spread out your background and ask the children to lay out the figures, their hats and any background details. When the children are happy with the arrangement, everything can be stuck on. You could also add items for the figures to hold.

**Making labels**: once your frieze is completed and pinned to the wall, sit down with the children and admire your work. You can then talk about the wording for a heading, to be written out and added to the display. As every child in the group will have participated, it is rather nice to put up each name - This picture was made by Jessica, Nazim, Charlie, Connor ....

The project described above is quite lengthy and complex. The different elements cater for a large number of children and a wide age range. Simplify the activity if your group is small and your children are younger.

Aim to provide as much flexibility within the structure of the activity as possible. For example, provide dark blue paint, printing objects and the body cut-outs and then let the children use the materials in their own way. Provide a range of different collage materials and then let the children choose how to add details to the uniform. Leave the children to decide whether they want to use chalk, wax or collage to make the faces.

**Assessment**

- ❑ The core of this activity is to explore the appearance of 'People who help us' through art and craft. Look out for how much visual detail the children notice and how well older ones can choose collage materials to represent the detail.
- ❑ The activity gives you a chance to see how children are using and consolidating the skills of printing, collage and drawing.
- ❑ This is a group activity with an end result produced by all the children working together. Observe how well the children co-operate and share the materials and tools.

# Planning for Creative Development

These pages explain how the 15 activities in this book cover the Early Learning Goals for Creative Development.

## Early Learning Goals for Creative Development

**ELG 1**: Explore colours, texture, shape, form and space in two or three dimensions.

**ELG 2**: Recognise and explore how sounds can be changed, sing simple songs from memory, recognise repeated sounds and sound patterns and match movements to music.

**ELG 3**: Respond in a variety of ways to what they see, hear, smell, touch and feel.

**ELG 4**: Use their imagination in art and design, music, dance, imaginative and role play and stories.

**ELG 5**: Express and communicate their ideas, thoughts and feelings by using a widening range of materials, suitable tools, imaginative and role play, movements, designing and making, and a variety of songs and musical instruments.

### Drawing (pages 20-23)

These activities help the development of pencil control and observational skills. 'Using different drawing materials' introduces the child to a range of drawing implements and techniques. Drawing media such as wax crayons and chalk encourage the children to explore colour and colour mixing. They also introduce to older children the idea of choosing media and colours for a particular purpose.

**Related goals: 1, 3, 4, 5**

### Printing (pages 24-25)

These activities introduce the skills needed to print successfully and help to develop fine motor movements and hand control. 'Printing patterns' helps the child to learn about pattern through giving her a simple technique for making her own patterns.

**Related goals: 1, 3, 4, 5**

### Collage (pages 26-29)

These activities introduce cutting and sticking and give the child the opportunity to practise and consolidate these fundamental skills. The range of materials that can be used for collage encourage the child to explore a variety of textures. Older children can experiment with and develop their understanding of composition through arranging the collage pieces before sticking. The activities also give the child the tools and skills she needs in order to express her thoughts and imagination through collage.

**Related goals: 1, 3, 4, 5**

### Modelling (pages 30-33)

The modelling activities enable the child to explore three-dimensional form through manipulating and moulding clay or playdough. 'Constructing models from junk' uses a number of art-related skills such as cutting, sticking and decorating techniques. Modelling also encourages the exploration of a variety of textures. The activities give the child the tools and skills she needs to express her thoughts and imagination through modelling and craft activities.

**Related goals: 1, 3, 4, 5**

### Beat out that rhythm! (pages 34-37)

These activities introduce the concept of rhythm through clapping and playing musical instruments. 'The beginnings of musical notation' introduces a simple technique for recording and composing rhythms. 'Making rhythms with body percussion' offers a different way of beating out rhythms and can be linked with a project on 'All about me'.

**Related goals: 2, 3, 4, 5**

### High, low, soft and loud (pages 38-41)

These activities introduce volume and pitch. They use speaking voices, singing voices and instruments. The 'Loud music, soft music' activity encourages the children to explore how sounds can be changed. 'The beginnings of musical notation' introduces a technique that enables older children to play simple tunes and compose and record their own sound pictures.

**Related goals: 2, 3, 4, 5**

**Exploring musical instruments (pages 42-45)**
These activities provide opportunities to explore different musical instruments, the ways in which they are played and the kind of music they create. Making a 'Musical instrument display' uses a variety of creative skills, including drawing, painting, model making and writing. Once the display is finished, the children can use it to further explore the instruments as part of their free play.

**Related goals: 1, 2, 3, 4, 5**

**Making musical instruments (pages 46-49)**
These activities use a number of art, craft and construction skills. Through making their own instruments, the children develop a greater understanding of the different ways in which sound can be created.

**Related goals: 1, 2, 3, 4, 5**

**Taste, touch and smell journeys (pages 50-53)**
Sensory experiences provide the information the child uses for all creative activities, from music to modelling. These activities focus on the senses of taste, touch and smell. They also encourage the communication of likes, dislikes and reactions to texture, taste and smell through language, facial expressions and gesture.

**Related goals: 1, 3, 5**

**Making up stories (pages 54-55)**
Making up stories is an important aspect of creativity. It is one of the main ways in which the child uses language creatively during the Foundation Stage. This activity gives the children a framework for creating and telling a group story, using narrative elements such as planning the ending, imagining the characters and deciding where the story takes place.

**Related goals: 4, 5**

**Seasons: Weather music (pages 56-59)**
These activities introduce the idea that music and dance can represent a theme. They also introduce the children to the idea of music as a communicative form. 'Playing weather music' enables the children to create their own representative sounds and explore the percussion instruments, including how to hold an instrument, get sound from it and change the nature of those sounds. Linking recorded music, dance and percussion instruments with a theme also gives the children new possibilities to use in expressing their creative thoughts and imagination.

**Related goals: 2, 3, 4, 5**

**Water: Miming (pages 60-61)**
Miming introduces the children to the concept of expressing thoughts and ideas through movement and gesture alone. The activities described here link with the theme of 'Water'. Through guessing what activity is being mimed, the group have to concentrate and interpret the movements. The mimer is encouraged to focus on mime as a form of communication as well as perform in front of the group.

**Related goals: 1, 3, 4, 5**

**Colour: Painting (pages 62-65)**
These activities introduce the child to the practical aspects of using a paint brush and easel. They encourage the child to explore and become familiar with paint, introducing a number of techniques for older children. 'Exploring colours' enables the child to experiment with mixing colour. 'Painting pebbles' introduces working on a small scale, producing an end result that can be treasured.

**Related goals: 1, 3, 4, 5**

**All about me: Circle dancing (pages 66-67)**
Circle dancing gives a clear dance format in which the child can learn and practise a variety of dance steps. It is a structured means of encouraging the children to move in rhythm to the music and it enables the child to explore body movements and space.

Circle dancing depends on group co-operation. This gives the child some useful opportunities to develop the ability to work in harmony with other people.

**Related goals: 1, 2, 4, 5**

**People who help us: Making a frieze (pages 68-69)**
This activity introduces working on a large scale. It also offers a means of making a group picture that every child can contribute to, regardless of age or skill level. Using a range of media and techniques introduces the idea that drawing, painting, printing and collage can be mixed together within the one picture.

**Related goals: 1, 3, 4, 5**

# Planning chart

| Creative Development | ELG 1 | ELG 2 | ELG 3 | ELG 4 | ELG 5 |
|---|---|---|---|---|---|
| Drawing | ✔ | | ✔ | ✔ | ✔ |
| Printing | ✔ | | ✔ | ✔ | ✔ |
| Collage | ✔ | | ✔ | ✔ | ✔ |
| Modelling | ✔ | | ✔ | ✔ | ✔ |
| Beat out that rhythm! | | ✔ | ✔ | ✔ | ✔ |
| High, low, soft, and loud | | ✔ | ✔ | ✔ | ✔ |
| Exploring musical instruments | ✔ | ✔ | ✔ | ✔ | ✔ |
| Making musical instruments | ✔ | ✔ | ✔ | ✔ | ✔ |
| Taste, touch and smell journeys | ✔ | | ✔ | | ✔ |
| Making up stories | | | | ✔ | ✔ |
| Seasons: Weather music | | ✔ | ✔ | ✔ | ✔ |
| Weather: Miming | ✔ | | ✔ | ✔ | ✔ |
| Colour: Painting | ✔ | | ✔ | ✔ | ✔ |
| All about me: Circle dancing | ✔ | ✔ | | ✔ | ✔ |
| People who help us: Making a frieze | ✔ | | ✔ | ✔ | ✔ |